HEALTH AND HUMAN DEVELOPMENT

MANAGED CARE IN A PUBLIC SETTING

HEALTH AND HUMAN DEVELOPMENT

JOAV MERRICK - SERIES EDITOR –

NATIONAL INSTITUTE OF CHILD HEALTH
AND HUMAN DEVELOPMENT,
MINISTRY OF SOCIAL AFFAIRS, JERUSALEM

Adolescent Behavior Research: International Perspectives
Joav Merrick and Hatim A. Omar (Editors)
2007. ISBN: 1-60021-649-8
(Hardcover)

Complementary Medicine Systems: Comparison and Integration
Karl W. Kratky
2008. ISBN: 978-1-60456-475-4
(Hardcover)
2008. ISBN: 978-1-61122-433-7
(E-book)

Pain in Children and Youth
Patricia Schofield and Joav Merrick (Editors)
2008. ISBN: 978-1-60456-951-3
(Hardcover)
2008. ISBN: 978-1-61470-496-6
(E-book)

Children and Pain
Patricia Schofield and Joav Merrick (Editors)
2009. ISBN: 978-1-60876-020-6
(Hardcover)
2009. ISBN: 978-1-61728-183-9
(E-book)

Challenges in Adolescent Health: An Australian Perspective
David Bennett, Susan Towns, Elizabeth Elliott and Joav Merrick (Editors)
2009. ISBN: 978-1-60741-616-6
(Hardcover)
2009. ISBN: 978-1-61668-240-8
(E-book)

Behavioral Pediatrics, 3rd Edition
Donald E. Greydanus, Dilip R. Patel, Helen D. Pratt and Joseph L. Calles, Jr. (Editors)
2009. ISBN: 978-1-60692-702-1
(Hardcover)
2009. ISBN: 978-1-60876-630-7
(E-book)

Health and Happiness from Meaningful Work: Research in Quality of Working Life
Søren Ventegodt and Joav Merrick (Editors)
2009. ISBN: 978-1-60692-820-2
(Hardcover)
2009. ISBN: 978-1-61324-981-9
(E-book)

Obesity and Adolescence:
A Public Health Concern
Hatim A. Omar, Donald E.
Greydanus, Dilip R. Patel
and Joav Merrick (Editors)
2009. ISBN: 978-1-60692-821-9
(Hardcover)
2009. ISBN: 978-1-61470-465-2
(E-book)

Poverty and Children:
A Public Health Concern
Alexis Lieberman and Joav Merrick
(Editors)
2009. ISBN: 978-1-60741-140-6
(Hardcover)
2009. ISBN: 978-1-61470-601-4
(E-book)

Alcohol-Related Cognitive
Disorders: Research and Clinical
Perspectives
Leo Sher, Isack Kandel
and Joav Merrick (Editors)
2009. ISBN: 978-1-60741-730-9
(Hardcover)
2009. ISBN: 978-1-60876-623-9
(E-book)

Conceptualizing Behavior in
Health and Social Research:
A Practical Guide to Data
Analysis
Said Shahtahmasebi
and Damon Berridge
2010. ISBN: 978-1-60876-383-2
(Hardcover)

Rural Child Health:
International Aspects
Erica Bell and Joav Merrick (Editors)
2010. ISBN: 978-1-60876-357-3
(Hardcover)
2010. ISBN: 978-1-61324-005-2
(E-book)

Living on the Edge: The
Mythical, Spiritual, and
Philosophical Roots of Social
Marginality
Joseph Goodbread
2009. ISBN: 978-1-60741-162-8
(Hardcover)
2011. ISBN: 978-1-61122-986-8
(Softcover)
2011. ISBN: 978-1-61470-192-7
(E-book)

Chance Action and Therapy:
The Playful Way of Changing
Uri Wernik
2010. ISBN: 978-1-60876-393-1
(Hardcover)
2011. ISBN: 978-1-61122-987-5
(Softcover)
2011. ISBN: 978-1-61209-874-6
(E-book)

Adolescence and Sports
Dilip R. Patel, Donald E. Greydanus,
Hatim Omar and Joav Merrick
(Editors)
2010. ISBN: 978-1-60876-702-1
(Hardcover)
2010. ISBN: 978-1-61761-483-5
(E-book)

**Advanced Cancer Pain
and Quality of Life**
*Edward Chow and Joav Merrick
(Editors)*
2011. ISBN: 978-1-61668-207-1
(Hardcover)
2010. ISBN: 978-1-61668-400-6
(E-book)

**Positive Youth Development:
Implementation of a Youth
Program in a Chinese Context**
*Daniel T.L Shek, Hing Keung Ma
and Joav Merrick (Editors)*
2011. ISBN: 978-1-61668-230-9
(Hardcover)

**Social and Cultural Psychiatry
Experience from the Caribbean
Region**
*Hari D. Maharajh and Joav Merrick
(Editors)*
2011. ISBN: 978-1-61668-506-5
(Hardcover)
2010. ISBN: 978-1-61728-088-7
(E-book)

**Narratives and Meanings
of Migration**
Julia Mirsky
2011. ISBN: 978-1-61761-103-2
(Hardcover)
2010. ISBN: 978-1-61761-519-1
(E-book)

**Self-Management and the Health
Care Consumer**
Peter William Harvey
2011. ISBN: 978-1-61761-796-6
(Hardcover)
2011. ISBN: 978-1-61122-214-2
(E-book)

**Sexology from a Holistic Point
of View**
Soren Ventegodt and Joav Merrick
2011. ISBN: 978-1-61761-859-8
(Hardcover)
2011. ISBN: 978-1-61122-262-3
(E-book)

**Principles of Holistic Psychiatry:
A Textbook on Holistic Medicine
for Mental Disorders**
Soren Ventegodt and Joav Merrick
2011. ISBN: 978-1-61761-940-3
(Hardcover)
2011. ISBN: 978-1-61122-263-0
(E-book)

**Clinical Aspects of
Psychopharmacology
in Childhood and Adolescence**
*Donald E. Greydanus, Joseph
L. Calles, Jr., Dilip P. Patel,
Ahsan Nazeer and Joav Merrick
(Editors)*
2011. ISBN: 978-1-61122-135-0
(Hardcover)
2011. ISBN: 978-1-61122-715-4
(E-book)

Climate Change and Rural Child Health
Erica Bell, Bastian M. Seidel and Joav Merrick (Editors)
2011. ISBN: 978-1-61122-640-9
(Hardcover)
2011. ISBN: 978-1-61209-014-6
(E-book)

Rural Medical Education: Practical Strategies
Erica Bell, Craig Zimitat and Joav Merrick (Editors)
2011. ISBN: 978-1-61122-649-2
(Hardcover)
2011. ISBN: 978-1-61209-476-2
(E-book)

Advances in Environmental Health Effects of Toxigenic Mold and Mycotoxins
Ebere Cyril Anyanwu
2011. ISBN: 978-1-60741-953-2
(Hardcover)

Child and Adolescent Health Yearbook 2009
Joav Merrick (Editor)
2011. ISBN: 978-1-61668-913-1
(Hardcover)

Public Health Yearbook 2009
Joav Merrick (Editor)
2011. ISBN: 978-1-61668-911-7
(Hardcover)

Child Health and Human Development Yearbook 2009
Joav Merrick
2011. ISBN: 978-1-61668-912-4
(Hardcover)

Alternative Medicine Yearbook 2009
Joav Merrick (Editor)
2011. ISBN: 978-1-61668-910-0
(Hardcover)

The Dance of Sleeping and Eating among Adolescents: Normal and Pathological Perspectives
Yael Latzer and Orna Tzischinsky (Editors)
2011. ISBN: 978-1-61209-710-7
(Hardcover)

Child and Adolescent Health Yearbook 2010
Joav Merrick (Editor)
2011. ISBN: 978-1-61209-788-6
(Hardcover)

Child Health and Human Development Yearbook 2010
Joav Merrick (Editor)
2011. ISBN: 978-1-61209-789-3
(Hardcover)

Public Health Yearbook 2010
Joav Merrick (Editor)
2011. ISBN: 978-1-61209-971-2
(Hardcover)

**Human Immunodeficiency Virus
(HIV) Research: Social Science
Aspects**
*Hugh Klein and Joav Merrick
(Editors)*
2012. ISBN: 978-1-62081-293-8
(Hardcover)

**Textbook on Evidence-Based
Holistic Mind-Body Medicine:
Research, Philosophy, Economy
and Politics of Traditional
Hippocratic Medicine**
*Søren Ventegodt and Joav Merrick
(Editors)*
2012. ISBN: 978-1-62257-140-6
(Hardcover)

**Textbook on Evidence-Based
Holistic Mind-Body Medicine:
Basic Philosophy and Ethics of
Traditional Hippocratic Medicine**
*Søren Ventegodt and Joav Merrick
(Editors)*
2012. ISBN: 978-1-62257-052-2
(Hardcover)

**Building Community Capacity:
Case Examples from Around the
World**
*Rosemary M. Caron
and Joav Merrick (Editors)*
2012. ISBN: 978-1-62417-175-8
(Hardcover)

**Building Community Capacity:
Skills and Principles**
*Rosemary M. Caron
and Joav Merrick (Editors)*
2012. ISBN: 978-1-61209-331-4
(Hardcover)

Public Health Yearbook 2011
Joav Merrick (Editor)
2012. ISBN: 978-1-62081-433-8
(Hardcover)

**Alternative Medicine Research
Yearbook 2011**
Joav Merrick (Editor)
2012. ISBN: 978-1-62081-476-5
(Hardcover)

Health Risk Communication
*Marijke Lemal and Joav Merrick
(Editors)*
2012. ISBN: 978-1-62257-544-2
(Hardcover)

HEALTH AND HUMAN DEVELOPMENT

MANAGED CARE IN A PUBLIC SETTING

RICHARD EVAN STEELE

New York

For permission to use material from this book please contact us:
Telephone 631-231-7269; Fax 631-231-8175
Web Site: http://www.novapublishers.com

NOTICE TO THE READER
The Publisher has taken reasonable care in the preparation of this book, but makes no expressed or implied warranty of any kind and assumes no responsibility for any errors or omissions. No liability is assumed for incidental or consequential damages in connection with or arising out of information contained in this book. The Publisher shall not be liable for any special, consequential, or exemplary damages resulting, in whole or in part, from the readers' use of, or reliance upon, this material. Any parts of this book based on government reports are so indicated and copyright is claimed for those parts to the extent applicable to compilations of such works.

Independent verification should be sought for any data, advice or recommendations contained in this book. In addition, no responsibility is assumed by the publisher for any injury and/or damage to persons or property arising from any methods, products, instructions, ideas or otherwise contained in this publication.

This publication is designed to provide accurate and authoritative information with regard to the subject matter covered herein. It is sold with the clear understanding that the Publisher is not engaged in rendering legal or any other professional services. If legal or any other expert assistance is required, the services of a competent person should be sought. FROM A DECLARATION OF PARTICIPANTS JOINTLY ADOPTED BY A COMMITTEE OF THE AMERICAN BAR ASSOCIATION AND A COMMITTEE OF PUBLISHERS.

Additional color graphics may be available in the e-book version of this book.

Library of Congress Cataloging-in-Publication Data

ISBN: 978-1-62417-970-9

Library of Congress Control Number: 2012956449

Published by Nova Science Publishers, Inc. † New York

CONTENTS

Foreword   xi
    Evelyne de Leeuw

Introduction   xiii
    Richard Evan Steele and Joav Merrick

Chapter 1   An introduction with theoretical background   1

Chapter 2   Operationalizing the strategy: An overview of the
process   11

Chapter 3   Operationalizing the strategy II: A spectrum of the
design and policy issues   15

Chapter 4   Overall policy and strategy   19

Chapter 5   Planning of projects and projected consequences   25

Chapter 6   Budgeting projects   35

Chapter 7   Planning the functions of CHC projects   39

Chapter 8   Projected operation of the CHC district   41

Chapter 9   Alternative limited implementation   47

Chapter 10   Evaluation of CHC projects   49

Chapter 11   Coordination and collaboration   59

Chapter 12   People with a disability in managed care   65
    Joav Merrick

Appendices   **83**

Appendix A   The literature study behind these guidelines   **85**

Appendix B   Project workshops/concept development   **87**

Appendix C   Political issues and project steering   **95**

Appendix D   Personnel profiles and development   **99**

Appendix E   Quality oriented service registration   **103**

Appendix F   Health profile and impact study   **107**

Appendix G   Community involvement   **111**

Acknowledgments   **113**

About the author   **115**

About Klinikken Livet   **119**

About the book series "Health and human development"   **121**

Index   **125**

FOREWORD

Professor Evelyne de Leeuw, MSc, MPH, PhD
Chair, Community Health Systems and Policy
School of Medicine, Deakin University, Victoria, Australia

Truths are never lost, they just get -occasionally- forgotten. Rick Steele's reflections on managed (primary) care are a powerful testimony to this.

In an age of ever-increasing hyper-specialisation in biomedical and clinical practice, of virtually logarithmic doubling of peer-reviewed health science literature every year, and of ever stronger beliefs around the pervasive nature of evidence-based health care, we have forgotten an important truth about people's health and how to care for it. Health is hardly created by the health system, which should rather be called the palliative system, or disease management system. Health, as the recent Marmot reviews on their social determinants show, is created where people live, love, work and play. Those places (or 'settings for health') are created and sustained by powerful systemic parameters, such as the economy, the ecosystem, education and early life, and most of all, political choice.

Managing this complex, interconnected, system of causes and 'causes of causes' of health and illness cannot be left to epidemiologists or clinicians, however brilliant they are.

Steele argues for a comprehensive, targeted and multi-professional approach to managed primary care that deals with some of the most challenging issues in the disease management system. His analysis stems from work mainly carried out in the 1980s and 1990s, and is strongly validated for the new millennium by two streams of action. First of all, Steele himself has been practicing his approach in a variety of capacities in Scandinavia for some decades now, yielding impressive results. But more importantly, recent insights and rediscoveries by WHO and other international and national bodies substantiate Steele's proposals. Recently, the World Health Assembly re-endorsed the Primary Health Care approach unequivocally, and not as a partial 'horizontal' or partial 'vertical' disease-driven community development strategy. Even more recently than that, a United Nations Summit was convened to address the looming - and in many places already rampant - epidemic of non-communicable disease. On both occasions, a measured and managed approach to health development and disease prevention was strongly advocated, and in turn endorsed by civil society.

Rick Steele isn't just rediscovering these truths. In his work he shows how to make it work.

INTRODUCTION

Richard Evan Steele, MD, MPH, PDC, BCSPHM[1],*
and Professor Joav Merrick, MD, MMedSci, DMSc[2],†
[1]Medical Director, Klinikken Livet, Denmark
[2]Medical Director, Health Services,
Division for Intellectual and Developmental Disabilities,
Ministry of Social Affairs and Social Services, Jerusalem, Israel

Health care has gone through profound changes in the preceding decades. Most of this change has been in what is possible clinically speaking. These changes have transgressed international boundaries by virtue of the international nature of and ease of access to the literature and the internationality of health care conferences and the use of the internet. Many different actors deserve credit for these developments, from individual doctors, nurses, therapists and innovators to local, regional, national and international health care organizations. Much change has also come about due to the migration of quality assurance thinking from industrial realms to health care. This has not been anywhere near as uniformly distributed as state of the art care, however. Even across centres of excellence for treatment of specific diseases, large differences in quality assurance can be found, and one can also

* Correspondence: Klinikken Livet, Tyttebærvej 26, Sejs, 8600 Silkeborg, Denmark; E-mail: steele@klinikken-livet.dk
† Correspondence: Health Services, Division for Intellectual and Developmental Disabilities, Ministry of Social Affairs and Social Services, POBox 1260, IL-91012 Jerusalem, Israel; E-mail: jmerrick@zahav.net.il

easily identify even more glaring deficiencies in quality of care in areas, where there is insufficient funding to make quality care available for all. Quality of care is augmented by the phenomenon called evidence based medicine, which for some conditions dictates a single clear treatment for specific conditions. In this as in many other areas of health care, a concept is utilized which goes far beyond its ability to stand up to a critical review. This is far more serious than most of us are willing to see in that overuse of a concept in health care invariably damages an unacceptably large proportion of patients instead of benefiting them. Even one case of treatment that does more harm than good is one too many. The true figures for this are not available, but it is estimated that they go as high as 20%, and a significant proportion of them cause unnecessary death (1).

The administration of health care is even more variable than quality of health care. This has many different reasons, not the least of which is traditional thinking. Other reasons include variability in the training of leadership, lack of relevant information on which to base decisions, a clear tendency to overuse new technology and the tendency for specialties to become more and more specific. Many decades ago, there were surgeons and internists. Now there are more than 50 specialties, and subspecialist categories are multiplying. There is a strong tendency for hospitalization as opposed to primary care in general, and this is good for a majority of the patients, but bad for a minority that is difficult to assess. Current patient record systems are not sensitized to this phenomenon and therefore data is not available, but this is likely the same approximately 20% mentioned above.

COORDINATION

In all health care systems there is a disturbing lack of coordination between various wards and specialties, between primary care and hospital care, between health care and social services and from sector to sector. There is furthermore so much more that could be done than is done in terms of dissemination of technology that it defies reason. This is mainly due to tradition. There is no area of health care, where this is more glaring than the overuse of hospital resources instead of upgrading and utilizing primary care, telemedicine and home care.

MANAGED CARE

Enter managed care. The general idea behind managed care is to maximize the health of the population served thus minimizing health care, while keeping costs down to a minimum. Previously, managed care organizations were called health maintenance organizations, or HMOs. A major hallmark of managed care is that it is capitated, meaning that the system has a fixed amount of cash for each person whether healthy or ill, under which all care is financed. This has many implications that could have a much greater impact than has been seen, yet the best examples of managed care offer significant advances in cost containment through minimization of hospitalization and simultaneous optimizing of primary care, while maintaining good quality of care and prioritizing health promotional activities. Certain aspects of managed care have received negative reporting, such as the so-called gag rules, where staff physicians are instructed not to tell patients about specific treatments, because they are viewed as being overly costly in spite of the relevance of the treatment. In spite of this, managed care has been reported as being at least as safe and quality ensured as traditional care, which in the US context means fee for service care. Under fee for service, payment is incurred as treatment is given, basically an open ended money generator. Obviously, fee for service plans have a monetary incentive to maximize treatment and little incentive to keep patients healthy. Indeed, there have been cases in which unneeded treatment was given for financial gain, and the US health care system is clearly much more expensive than publicly funded systems. It must be stated that various systems have been attempted to reign in these costs, most notable of which are the Medicaid and Medicare cost containment stipulations and the phenomenon known as diagnosis related groups specifying a fixed payment level for at given diagnosis. It may seem hard to understand that fee for service continues to exist when a managed care alternative is available, but here again, tradition plays the major role. There remains a belief that fee for service plans offer greater choice and flexibility, although it has not been shown that this is so.

Publicly funded health care systems, which are much more widespread than private health care systems internationally, all function in principle as capitated systems, and should be easily managed as HMOs.

In spite of the logic behind this, managed care in its coordinating and cost containment roles has only just scratched the surface of publicly funded systems. There are great advances to be made in coordination of care and services, effectuating the lowest effective level of care, ensuring quality of care, minimizing costs and promoting health. The complex of barriers to such advances is tough and rugged, but with political courage and creativity, enormous results can be achieved. This is especially relevant in countries with high proportions of the population on publicly funded income, notably northern Europe. In other words, the higher the disease rate, whether it be medical or social, the greater the potential for positive development.

REFERENCES

[1]   Kohn LT, Corrigan JM, Donaldson MS, eds. To err is human: Building a safer health system. Washington, DC: National Academy Press, 2000.

Chapter 1

AN INTRODUCTION WITH THEORETICAL BACKGROUND

If one were to pool all of the resources tied to health and social services in a given community and had the opportunity to plan the delivery of health and social services with no limitations on the way these were planned except the sum total of resources, would the resulting system look like anything we know today? Although this may sound like a preposterous proposition, thinking this way is nonetheless the only way to achieve movement towards an optimal system. I have not met one individual with whom I have shared this thought who did not immediately recognize the potential for seriously positive development based on such a strategy. The question then arises, "What are we waiting for?" These guidelines are designed as a manual for moving in that direction with sound argumentation for most aspects of what this strategy could come up against from opponents who think that tradition should prevail.: In these guidelines, the following will be covered:

- An introduction with theoretical background
- Operationalizing the strategy, an overview of the process
- Operationalizing the strategy II, a spectrum of the design and policy issues
- Overall policy and strategy
- Planning of projects and projected consequences
- Budgeting the project
- Planning the functions of CHC projects
- Projected operation of the CHC district
- Alternative limited implementation

- Evaluation of CHC projects
- Coordination and collaboration
- Appendix A – The literature study behind these guidelines
- Appendix B – Project workshops/concept development
- Appendix C – Political issues and project steering
- Appendix D –Personnel profiles and development
- Appendix E – Quality oriented service registration
- Appendix F – Health profile and impact study
- Appendix G – Community involvement

In spite of all the differences that exist from country to country in the delivery of health care, there is a remarkable similarity among health care systems in industrialized countries with respect to three major areas:

- Coordination of care: All of these systems display a disconcerting lack of coordination between sectors, notably between the social and health sectors but also between the primary and hospital sectors and internally within the sectors. The conceptual framework of this paper is that given the sheer size and diversity of the typical functional units currently delivering health care, optimal coordination from the patient's point of view is inherently unachievable, unless one adapts the concepts described below,
- quality development and improvement: The health impact of health systems is poorly documented and what little data does exist is indicative of definite deficiencies. The timely and quality oriented registration of services is still rudimentary and needs considerable development before significant advances can be made, and
- management of health services: There are in all of these systems serious problems with management, the most obvious and serious effect of which is the issue of constantly rising real costs. The size of budgets and personnel groups common in these systems make them practically unmanageable, and all too few health system administrators are willing or able to communicate effectively with health services staff.

These deficiencies in the health care systems in industrialized countries have been increasingly under fire for decades. In the newspapers, radio, television, public meetings, etc. one hears comments like "Something has to be done," more and more often. Even in biomedical journals, where one would not normally expect to find such diatribes, a large number of editorials and correspondences have questioned the dominant trends in health care delivery systems. The word crisis has often been used. One commonly propounded argument is that hospital care has outstripped its role, and that a large scale roll back to primary care is in order. The concept of community oriented primary care (COPC) is still on the cutting edge of this development, even though the concept as such is not new. Basically, COPC is a melding of health care and public health. In this context, the patient oriented service concept is central, with the system built around community needs as expressed through community as well as individual diagnoses. Planning, implementation, and evaluation in COPC are carried out in a cyclical pattern, denoting an ongoing process, whereby continuity and development are ensured. An overview of COPC is obtained from Conner and Mullan, editors (1). A newer, more practically oriented collection is offered by Nutting, editor (2). Abramson (3) gives a review of the literature and planning developments in COPC. These guidelines take all of this into account and go the one step further to create a comprehensive state of the art primary care system denoted comprehensive health care, or CHC.

The bulk of the literature on this subject comes from the United States. A great part of this literature has arisen from efforts to alleviate the problems of the underserved, uninsured or indigent population in the US, and has thus been concentrated on primary care. On the surface it would seem that the conditions for community oriented primary care would be non-conducive in the US, where the health care system is predominated by market forces. On the other hand, the emergence in the US of competition in health care services delivery has given community oriented primary care a new significance (4,5). Furthermore, the problem of the uninsured in the US population as well as the high administrative costs and the difficulties with vertical service integration has given rise to a number of proposals for a national health insurance system in the US. Among the more prominent of these was the Califano proposal under the Carter administration, which never got out of committee, the American Physicians for a National Health Program (6), a bipartisan commission (Pepper) on health care and a host of independent organization and state proposals for universal health care coverage in the US. In all of these proposals, advanced primary care plays a central role. More recently, the Obama administration developed and got through congress the proposal for an Affordable Health Care Act, which as its main agenda had as the insuring of the approximately 45 million American citizens without health care insurance at an affordable rate. Even though the Supreme Court has put down protests against this legislation, its future remains uncertain in that the Republicans, if they win a majority in Congress and the presidency, have vowed to roll back this legislation (7).

The guidelines below present detailed guidelines for developing CHC designed to address the above issues. One of the guiding principles behind the guidelines is that only through a cyclical, formal planning process involving detailed knowledge of the target population can a rational delivery system for primary care be devised. This is also the central thesis of COPC from earlier works (8). Meanwhile, the limitation of COPC, as has been implemented so far, to the primary sector makes it unsuitable as a system strategy. These guidelines define a form of health service delivery which is viable within a larger context.

The guidelines include but are not limited to primary care, and the ensuing system would cover the totality of health care for a defined population while resting on the principles of community orientation in all possible respects. At the same time, projects adhering to these guidelines would test many of the central tenets of the WHO Health for All 2020 strategy, of which community oriented primary care may be said to be a part. For the purpose of these guidelines, this strategy would be termed comprehensive health care (CHC).

Various solutions to the 3 main problems described in the introduction have been attempted. A WHO-EURO technical committee meeting in England was devoted to describing and discussing these proposals and experiences. Country reports were presented from 11 European countries (Meeting ICP/MPN 039, Jan. 29-31, 1990, project officer Dr. Rafael Bengoa, WHO-EURO office). Striking similarities exist in these developments, the major themes revolving around coordination of services and quality of care and incentives for reaching these, i.e. good management principles. One major conclusion of the meeting was that insufficient knowledge existed to make relevant system strategy proposals. Experimentation with innovative designs and research in existing projects is therefore needed. This was painfully clear in 1990, and what has happened in the meantime is more to the detriment of such thinking than furthering development. There is little clarity on the why of this lack of development, but in my view, there can be little doubt that the constant turf and budget battles that have plagued health care since then are the main culprits.

In several countries, developments directed towards CHC have been underway for a number of years. Developments of this nature have been analyzed for their usefulness in developing these guidelines. For example, in

Finland, a government white paper of 1972 placed this concept centrally in the planning of the future health care system, and the result is a unique system placing the planning responsibility for community health in the community. This system has had many positive effects on community health, a good example of which is the North Karelia coronary heart disease project. A review of ten years of experience from this project is given by Puska et al (8). A number of problems continue to face the system, however, not the least of which is the estrangement of the local and central planning systems. At the community level, there is planning responsibility but little or no budgetary influence. Saltman (10) gives a perceptive account of this development and the probable immediate future of the Finnish system. Other countries have similar developments planned and/or underway, e.g. the overhaul of the British National Health Service under the parole of "Working for Patients". The government white paper and its attendant documents (11) call for and describe large scale organizational changes aimed at increasing the community orientation of the British National Health Service.

Another body of literature analyzed arises from a number of management issues pertaining attempts to maximize quality and minimize cost in health care, with the main emphasis on containing cost. Enthoven is often given credit for breaking the ground in this connection with a very often quoted paper commissioned by the British National Health Service in 1985 (12). In this paper, Enthoven espouses the concept of the internal market, later called managed competition (13). Saltman and van Otter expand on this theme (14) proposing a public health care system in which market mechanisms would play a dominant role. Saltman and van Otter fall short of describing how this would work at the district or local level, however. These guidelines take the opposite track, defining the system from the local level and describing the macro level on that background.

A third body of writings utilized in the development of these guidelines is the strategic writings known as Health for All by the year 2000 (HFA2000) developed by WHO and its regional secretariats. In the documents surrounding HFA2000, the central theme is social justice (15-24). This body of work describes in some detail what a health care system year 2000 should have looked like in the form of political goals. The writings do not give much guidance as to how to achieve this health system. One useful concept arising from this material is that poor coordination and lack of community orientation is not only socially unjust, but is also bad business. Meanwhile, the issue of universal health goals has been one of the many casualties of the political upheavals of the last several decades, where social justice has not been on the front burner. The resulting lack of cohesion in writings from the WHO has reflected this in a hodgepodge of relatively uncoordinated goals for 2020.

A fourth body of literature utilized has been the description of the US phenomenon known as the health maintenance organization (HMO). The HMO concept is central to the financial strategy behind these guidelines, and a brief background of this phenomenon is therefore given below. The basic concept in the HMO philosophy can be said to be capitated prepayment (as opposed to cost as incurred) and the integration of the financing and provision of health services. These two basic concepts serve in principle to maximize the incentives for keeping those insured healthy, hence the name health maintenance organization. If one were to stop the description here, the typical European public health care system could be described as an HMO. Most European countries organize their health care systems around some or other regionalization scheme, with regional tax and political authorities having the responsibility for a large proportion of the total health care budget for the region's population. The yearly budget acts in effect like a prepayment scheme. Unlike the HMO where the premium paid goes directly to and only to health care and the administration of health care (and profit, where applicable), the budgets in European public health care systems are tax based and can grow or diminish without any direct connection to the actual cost of health care. Health care budgets in such systems are part of a larger overall tax scheme, so that savings or budgetary overflows are not necessarily felt by the payers or the providers.

HMOs are however, more than a budgetary or financial arrangement. In their search for cost containment or profits while keeping integrity of care within acceptable standards, HMOs use a myriad assortment of incentives, coverage plans, risk sharing and cost accounting schemes. The diversity of institutions calling themselves HMOs is enormous. In the words of American managed care researcher JP Weiner, "When you have seen one HMO, you have seen one HMO." In a Kings Fund Institute paper, Weiner and his associate D Ferris explore the financial arrangements of HMOs as relates to the British National Health Service. The authors also provide a brief history of HMOs as pertains to the British Working for Patients strategy as well as an excellent literature list which can serve as an appetizer for the interested reader (25). A more complete historical overview than Weiner and Ferris offer is provided by B. Abel-Smith (26) or John A Nelson (27).

In the last 40 years or so, the prime mover in HMO development has been cost containment and/or profit-making. Inter study (28) data indicate that approximately 60% of the present HMO plans are for profit organizations, while approximately 50% of the total enrollees are covered by for profit plans. Clearly, a for-profit plan in open competition with public or non-profit organizations has maximized incentives for keeping operating costs down. This argument is flawed when applied to the US system, however, since cost containment there has failed (29), an anomaly which many authors fail to address. HMOs utilize various methods to achieve cost containment. These include gatekeeping to minimize unnecessary utilization, utilization review with risk sharing, advanced accounting systems and to some extent vertical integration of services. This is where the main differences between an efficient HMO and the typical European public health care district lie. The main contribution of the HMO literature in this context its significant input to the management issues addressed here.

Before leaving this short discussion of the HMO concept, mention must be made of the debate which has raged around the theme that efficient management in health care can be dangerous to your health. The literature is not wholly conclusive on this front, but the majority of the studies underpin the overall integrity of managed care as a provider. Weiner states, "It is generally accepted that when compared to fully insured people receiving care under fee for service, persons under the care of doctors in HMOs receive more ambulatory and preventive care, and from 10 to 40 percent less hospital care (due to lower admission rates). Overall, the savings are estimated to be in the 5 to 30 percent range." Luft (30) and Hillman (31) have described the economic incentive mechanisms by which these savings are attained, and more recently, Hillman (32) describes the apparent effectiveness of these incentives to modify physician behaviour. Despite the significant savings, Ware et al. (33) (from the Rand material), Weiner (34), Wouldiamson (35) and Luft (36) find it documented that HMOs provide at least as safe and quality level care as fee for service health care delivery systems. The quality of care issue is developed more fully below.

The combination of the above described developments and strategies and the emergence of data defending the integrity of quality of care in managed, for profit health care has given rise to speculation that a common end point may be found, i.e. the public competition model or internal market. A major weakness in the development of this system strategy is a lack of empirical knowledge about how a system incorporating the best of both worlds would work. The concepts need to be operationalized at the level of service delivery. The system strategy which arises from this conceptual operationalization involves so many aspects of health care delivery that the adoption of such a strategy at a regional or national level is hardly feasible. This is especially true when regarding the possibilities for a valid and reliable evaluation of the envisaged system. This would be extremely difficult in the development of a CHC institution, and probably impossible in a system upheaval. National strategy development could profit enormously from projects designed to pilot these concepts aided by research to implement a transitional strategy at the regional/national level.

These guidelines are defined with a background in the Northern European setting, more specifically in Denmark (for this reason a number of Scandinavian language references, which generally have English language summaries, have been included). These guidelines can be utilized to establish a community and/or an administrative health care entity that is delineable from other communities/administrative entities. This is necessary in order to limit the budget, risk and inclusion criteria for a health district devised under these guidelines. Traditional real and imagined barriers between community, primary, secondary and tertiary services would be systematically and willfully broken down. The intention is to give the district sufficient flexibility to make possible a system in which all of the players, from the health authority director to the sick and disabled patient, act under a supplemental or at the least non conflicting set of incentives to reach the best possible service or treatment close to or in the patient's home and for the least possible cost.

One example of how such a set of common incentives could work is in the area of home care and extended community services (described extensively below). The best possible care in the home setting, when this is feasible, costs less than half of what a comparable care costs in an in-patient hospital setting. Although there is very little literature documenting this, the few existing papers are quite forceful in their conclusions, e.g. Clarke's Hospital at Home (37) and Steele's "A novel and effective treatment modality for medically unexplained symptoms" (38). In other words, this strategy would open up an economic window of opportunity for resources to become available for alternative uses. A precondition for this happening is of course that the system actually works, and in order to ensure this, a number of incentive systems must be devised. One such is the contractual referral service, the scheme for the drafting of which is sketched in appendix B of these guidelines. In the first of a planned series of workshops, the participants would be asked to find 40% of the internal medicine bed days and 25% of the surgical bed days which can be taken care of in the primary sector. This gives a rough idea of the size of the resources that become mobile under this strategy.

The planning process for projects developed under these guidelines is expected to give a large number of spin-off effects which can be utilized within existing health system structures. This is an indirect benefit of the strategic planning process which would be available long before the envisaged system could be implemented. The planning process would provide extensive information about system structure and process which would not have been available before. Such information would allow a maximal rationalization of that same service within its existing context. Examples of this type of mechanism can be found in improved cost/benefit in fee for service systems in the US which became possible because of the information gathered on effective incentive systems used in HMOs. There can also be no doubt that a concerted effort to find a way to eradicate the boundaries between the sectors would facilitate inter-sectoral cooperation.

Being that roughly 70% of the running costs of hospitals go to personnel wages, any reduction in hospital capacity would necessarily be accompanied by personnel reductions in that sector. It is quite probable that it would be possible to rationalize the general use of personnel with overall reductions in certain categories as a result. This can be seen both as a good and a bad situation. Good because it raises the possibility of overall savings at the system level and frees up highly qualified individuals for other needed activities and bad because it would be likely to cause significant disruption and unrest in the health care labour market. It would depend on the courage and especially the phantasy of responsible politicians and managers to make use of the opportunities thus provided, using the mobilized personnel e.g. on prevention projects, community outreach activities, needed research etc. It would be fatal to underestimate the significance of this problem, especially as regards the active cooperation needed on the part of the health care personnel to make the system work. Personnel incentives have therefore received high priority in these guidelines, see below under "Budgeting projects."

Chapter 2

OPERATIONALIZING THE STRATEGY: AN OVERVIEW OF THE PROCESS

The transition from the strategic statements to functional implementation of CHC projects would entail a progressively more complex set of actors, knowledge and projections as they near functionality. This section gives an overview of the expected process of this transition. The preparatory stage of the project necessitates a good deal of research and planning. The initial phases of this process would lead to the decision-making process on the part of politicians and/or financial backers to go ahead with the implementation of the envisaged system or simply reap the benefits of the spin-off effects of the planning process. Obviously, full benefit of the planning process described requires project implementation.

THE DESIGN PHASE

During this time, information would have been gathered on the state of the art in a number of research areas and methods of practice/delivery with relevance to project function. These are described in detail below. This can be accomplished through an in-depth literature study, site visits and a review network. In appendix A, a short description of the working methods for these activities is provided. Also during this phase the potential players in the project must be identified: who is committed, who supports the project, who is against it, which organizations must be contacted, are any exceptions from existing laws necessary, etc. This preliminary stage would end when a decision by a relevant health authority is made to launch the project, leading to a more concrete, localized planning phase.

THE PLANNING/METHODOLOGY PHASE

This phase would be characterized by "tooling up" for the implementation of the project system. This would entail adapting the project to local conditions and gathering the experiences to be had from relevant local and regional authorities in the field. The planning, implementing and evaluative tools would be developed further. The following list of problem areas must be handled in the preliminary phase, others need further development as research or practice areas and still others must await the concrete planning process before they can take form.

A pricing system for health care activities. This would allow the mobilization of resources involved in transferring an activity/service from one sector to another. This includes actual price strategies and the physical ordering of the transfer system. Within the US context, this is relatively clear-cut, even though the transition as such may not be so straightforward. In European countries, this would be groundbreaking work.

A management information system (MIS) strategy. This can draw to some extent on existing database technology, but serious deficiencies still exist within this context. This is a typical example of an aspect of the planning process which would have spin-off effects for the health care system in general. The MIS must integrate clinical management, accountability, quality and communications.

An evaluation strategy. This can provide ongoing information on the health impact of the project, including community diagnosis.

A development system for leadership style and tools for effectuating an effective steering and evaluation of the referral and incentive systems, see subsequent sections.

Development and adoption of educational tools to act as standalone incentives for personnel as well as preparing personnel for the many different tasks which would diverge from the mainstream of present delivery systems.

Development and collection of research tools which can elucidate the nature of project development process as well as translating the knowledge gained from running the project into a framework suitable for general system policy making. Such research tools would be dependent on and act as incentives for recruitment of professionals with basic epidemiological as well as high quality clinical skills to work in the project.

IMPLEMENTATION PHASE

After the decision to launch a concrete, localized planning process, the development of the project protocol would take approximately one year. This version of the guidelines is based on the literature and the experience of the author with health policy workshops in Europe. The scope of the guidelines is of course limited by the lack of previous history of this type of system. When fully developed during a localized planning process, the protocol would include detailed plans for the functions of the CHC district (*inter alia* by virtue of the referral code, i.e. the rules regarding which patients are retained in the primary setting and which patients need hospital admission), its relations to the general health care system, personnel profiles and manpower needs, educational and personnel development strategy, the budget, organization, technology and physical needs. While developing the protocol, attention must be paid to the possibility that the system may never be realized. The spin-off effects of the planning process would then be the main advantage.

CONSOLIDATION/EVALUATION

The characteristics of this phase would depend on what happens after the localized planning phase. If the system is implemented, the major emphasis of the evaluation would be placed on the health impact of implemented projects. This would be an integral part of the documentation necessary to give impetus to regional and/or national system development based on this thinking. It is therefore not expected to be overly taxing on the pilot system personnel, as the system would be designed to follow the health of the community both *a priori* and *a posteriori*. Depending on the outcome of this evaluation and the political developments in the meantime, the project would be continued, duplicated, reduced or abandoned. In any case, the impact on the general system strategy and regional health policy would be evaluated. In the event that the pilot system is not implemented after the localized planning phase, an evaluation of the health impact of the planning process itself would be attempted, as the planning process per se is intended to activate the community in a number of health related areas.

Pilot systems that are implemented would require an end-point evaluation after 5-7 year time span. The process must encompass all relevant authorities and as a minimum include the following:

1. The national health committee
2. The Ministry of Health
3. The Board of Health
4. The Hospital Institute (where relevant)
5. Relevant Regional Councils
6. Relevant municipality councils
7. Relevant Universities
8. Relevant hospitals and group practices which could be candidates for the project itself
9. The national associations of physicians, nurses, therapists, psychologists, etc.
10. WHO

Chapter 3

OPERATIONALIZING THE STRATEGY II: A SPECTRUM OF THE DESIGN AND POLICY ISSUES

Whereas the last chapter gave an overview of what could be called the internal planning process for projects following these guidelines, this chapter outlines the major design and policy issues that would require political and central management involvement. As described above, the purpose of projects under these guidelines is to test a number of theories concerning the organization of health care service delivery. The pilot system coming out of this theoretical framework is expected to elasticize the delivery system, increase service quality and the general accessibility of services while improving the health status of the target population. Projects would involve the creation of a health district with a population base of approximately 10-20,000 persons. The district would have the sum total responsibility for all health and social needs pertaining to that population, some of which would be taken care of within the district and some of which would be obtained elsewhere, mainly hospitalization with the reductions described above. In the event the project entails a hospital closing, a new visitation plan must be conceived. The why and wherefore of this organization would become clear as the project planning progresses.

Placement of the project is potentially problematical. A number of considerations are relevant in this connection. In order to maximize the generalizability of the conclusions of project evaluation, the target population must be reasonably representative of regional or national norms, i.e. not outlying in terms of health or social issues. The project must be positively received locally. The district in question must be positioned administratively in the geographical area such that the relocation and/or mobilization of services and resources are practicable and meaningful. Ideally, this would probably equate to a district in which a small hospital was under devolution or a rural district in which a large group practice was already in place. The local administration would be sensitized to the resource/services mobilization process in both cases.

The budget of the project is intended to include community health and preventive services and social services, the primary medical sector and a standardized per capita hospital budget. As such, the CHC health authority would have budgetary freedom for all aspects of health care for the district population, although within certain bounds which are discussed in some detail below. For example, treatments already exempted from local/regional fiscal responsibility would of course continue to be so under the project's budget, typically haemophiliacs, transplantation patients, etc. The actual budgeting process would be quite complex and fraught with uncertainties.

From a macro-economical point of view, the most important aspect of projects created under these guidelines is the intended creation of a comprehensive system of incentives which promote the use of the lowest effective level of care. The district must pay for centralized hospital services, which creates a direct negative incentive to use hospital services and an equally direct positive incentive to utilize and increase local services. Without steering mechanisms, this would tend to lead to the creation of micro hospitals, which most likely would lead to more costly and less rational delivery of services. This is naturally not what is intended. It is also of utmost importance that projects do not entail a lowering of the service level in the community, especially pertaining to the frail or elderly. That some less effective services may be discontinued is another matter. The steering mechanism which the pilot system would utilize is a contractual referral system with budgetary ramifications. The referral system would also protect the district delivery system from getting bogged down by long term patients while ensuring a minimum level of service quality. In order to be workable, this referral system must be conceived and condoned as close to the actors in the system as possible. The forum needed for this work can be found in the workshop method, in which system actors and administrators work out the system together. The methodology ensures that all participants are oriented about the developments while accepting at least some level of responsibility for the plan. The needed workshops are described in appendix B.

A central issue in the administrative context is what level of utilizable information concerning system strategy can be generated through project development. This is intended as a top priority for the project administration, and the MIS which would run under the project would be optimized for cross sectional and longitudinal analysis in the largest possible number of free combinations. The information generated would be analyzed with respect to health impact, economics and logistics, trade agreement conditions, training and educational conditions including what effect the project has on professional/patient roles and what areas of research are facilitated or inhibited by the project. This analysis would be made available publicly through a series of reports accessible to the lay person. Beyond that, it is expected that the project would stimulate a number of research projects which would greatly enhance the information value of the projects.

Chapter 4

OVERALL POLICY AND STRATEGY

Development of these guidelines has been based on a strategic planning process started as a consultancy for the Funen District Health Authority in Denmark and then as a research project during two research/study years at the Johns Hopkins University School of Hygiene and Public Health funded by the Danish Research Academy and IbHenriksen's Fund.

This study time afforded the research behind these guidelines and time for reflection on a more pragmatic conceptualization of how all of this could work. In the following text, a large number of questions rising out of the theoretical considerations are given form and solutions are sketched in more or less detail. It is expected that the main body of this work would remain intact as planning processes proceed, but it is also expected that planning processes would give most of the problem areas considerably more body and the solutions greater operationality. The goal formulation for the pilot system which arises from the theoretical background for projects and their policy basis are dealt with below.

The preparatory stage of the project is to a large extent a desk oriented job. The work cut out is to operationalize the above considerations in a form which can give body to a live project locally. Most of this work has been done as preparation for these guidelines, and therefore does not need to be repeated. This has led to the production of a number of scenarios describing likely outcomes for each major problem area.

The greatest advantages of this work are the three pillars of comprehensive health care: coordination of care, quality of care and management of health services. The operationalization of the three concepts in system strategy has followed a natural path translating the concepts into a statement of objectives. This has happened throughout a series of health policy workshops run by the project designer in seven European countries. The two headings that this statement of objectives falls under are continuous quality development (CQD) and the lowest effective level of care (LELOC). These two headings transcend the boundaries between the three issues such that a comprehensive strategy can be designed. This will be clarified below.

As areas of professional endeavour, both CQD and LELOC are relatively new, and certainly not universally in use or accepted. We have not yet been able to systematize our knowledge in these areas and take due consequence. Indeed, the concepts are still having a hard time getting over the definitional stage. Vuori (39) gives some excellent insights into CQD from the WHO perspective, broadly defining CQD as an activity ensuring that health services do more good than harm. CQD theory in policy terms is presented, but Vuori's work leaves the reader with a feeling that little has been accomplished, and much needs to be done. More practical suggestions are offered in two WHO EURO documents on CQD (40,41). An overall CQD framework at the policy level is provided in European targets for Health for All (42), especially targets 31 and 38. A good overview of CQD methodology, both in the hospital and primary sector, is provided in a recent quasi-governmental Swedish document (43). In the US, the CQD literature is much further along in terms of operationalization, but the special circumstances surrounding the US health care situation make generalizing the applicability of this information outside the US very complicated. Donabedian (44) has provided a number of excellent conceptual pieces integrating CQD into the mainstream of American hospital administration theory. Goldfield and Nash (45) provide an excellent overview of the US CQD literature (mostly hospital based) and present a large number of examples of how specific CQD activities work in their respective settings. Operational strategy frameworks applicable at the local level have been attempted in several cases (46, 47, 48). While CQD is becoming a reasonably well documented concept area, studies providing insight into the LELOC concept come from a much broader framework. As discussed in the introduction, a number of studies document the efficiency of managed care as a means of reducing hospitalization rates within HMOs, but this is only reducing a level which is grossly overemphasized to begin with. The LELOC concept demands that one find the actual limitations for the level of care and effectuate a policy which maximizes the incentives for maintaining that level. A related area which has received little research attention but much attention from payers of health care in the US setting is utilization review (UR). UR is basically a set of criteria designed to limit inappropriate use of health care services in an attempt to contain runaway costs, while quality issues often take a back seat. A review of the UR literature is not achievable still because of the lack of quality research. Kemper (49,50), however, offers a quality oriented methodology for UR in a pediatrics setting. More documentation for UR can be found in American managed care handbooks and hospital accreditation guidelines, e.g. Kongstvedt (51), or in business oriented evaluations of UR, e.g. Vibbert (52). Large scale studies designed to explore the LELOC issue in a CQD oriented context have not appeared in the literature, and if an operational LELOC strategy framework has been formulated, it does not seem to have been published.

The problem that these concepts address is the barrier between the hospital sector and the primary sector. For moderately to severely ill patients, the primary care physician (PCP) often does not have access to a viable alternative to hospital admission, even though hospital care as such may not be necessary or desired. There is a large gap from where the capabilities of the primary sector leave off and the capabilities of the hospital sector begin. This gap is demonstrated by the hospital in-patients who could have been treated in the primary sector if only some basic prerequisites concerning availability of nursing and medical support were fulfilled. This problem is perpetrated by institutional limitations. Such limits are found internally in hospitals, e.g. between medical and surgical departments, between hospitals and the primary medical sector, between hospitals and community nursing services and between the health sector and the social sector.

The background for these limitations is complex, and it is not meant to deal extensively with this background here. Let it suffice to say that a significant part of the in-patient pressure on hospitals can be extracted directly from the barrier between the hospitals and the primary medical sector on one hand and between the primary medical sector and community nursing services on the other. This situation often works to the detriment of both the system and the patient, as e.g. when insufficient availability of home nursing is the only significant factor in a hospital admission (or in an overlong in-patient length of stay), or an increase in nosocomial infections. The situation is of course entirely different in a health care market with a hospital bed glut, which is the case in certain American, and curiously, Russian cities (53).

A number of studies provide insight into the significance of this problem, both in terms of patients or bed day equivalents and in financial terms. However, it is quite clear that the limits for home care/primary sector care are not known, and that these limits are certainly well beyond normal practice. In other words, much more could be done in the home and community setting than now is done, both in terms of quantity and quality. In the Danish context, studies to ascertain the proportion of theoretically unnecessary hospital admissions have produced figures of 15-40% of patient bed days (54-56). In the US literature, the figures go as high as 60% (57-60). Caution must be taken in comparing these figures, as the American figures are mainly based on situations where underserved populations have been offered wholly new services. Still, the tendency seems clear. The actual figure would always fluctuate, it being a product of availability of hospital beds, availability of financial resources, technology, availability of nursing services, attitudes of medical personnel and exclusiveness of professional agreements. In other words, it is largely up to one's phantasy to set a limit on the capabilities of the primary sector.

Meanwhile, some or other figure must be used, as this is the basis for a number of strategic processes, including hospital budgeting, referral systems, ambulance services etc. In order to find a figure which is different from the empirical value, it is necessary to devise an operational target system. The targets must adhere to national and international policy as well as taking local/regional considerations into account. The following target system, or reference frame, is based on the literature cited, the Danish government prevention program (61) a collection of health policy related examples from the Danish Ministry of Health (62) and WHO's Health for All targets (63). In other words, all of the relevant policy documents have been taken into account as they pertain to the Danish health care system, under which these guidelines have been developed. Obviously, similar collection and analysis of national, regional and local laws, rules and regulations relevant in the project area/locality needs to be carried out during the planning process. The resulting targets are more or less relevant in most countries and settings, needing only modest editing under local conditions. Furthermore, the reference frame is intentionally limited to those areas of these policy statements which deal with system organization and quality assurance, and the statements are couched in terms applicable in practical planning.

The reference frame is divided into two main headings mirroring LELOC and CQD. The two resulting lists overlap to some extent, but are formulated such that the LELOC list is primarily targeted at the system level the CQD list is primarily targeted at the institutional level. The LELOC list

- The best possible care close to the patient's home and for the lowest possible expenditure.
- A health system based on the needs and wishes of the community as expressed through a community diagnosis,

- The health problems of the patient must be approached in a holistic fashion, which is best accomplished through an inter professional approach,
- All interventions must take place as close as possible to the patient's home based on social, economic and medical priorities in that order, unless special circumstances dictate otherwise,
- The patient must not experience institutional limitations during the intervention, e.g. a lengthened hospital stay because of unavailable home care,
- Specialist treatment and consultation must be equally available to all,
- All interventions must be conducted at the appropriate professional level, taking into consideration that early warning signs of serious disease must be discovered when possible.
- Hospitals must be reserved for the very ill and those who need intensive care and treatment. This entails the adoption of a set of criteria: For example, hospital care is reserved for patients requiring constant medical attention, needing attention of two or more persons simultaneously or needing direct observation more than half hourly,
- The health system must be able to document a positive health impact in all but marginal cases, including minimizing the impact of poor health on the work force, and
- The health system must make its position clear to the public, so that the public expectations and the capabilities of the system concur as much as possible.

The CQD list: It must be documentable that each and every intervention conducted by the health system does more good than harm to the patient:

- In health education, the institution must imbibe the patient with sufficient information about their condition in order to facilitate the best possible decision concerning the course of the interventions,
- Clinical care must be coordinated, competent and documented,
- The interventions must be morally, ethically and personally acceptable to the patient, and as convenient and accessible as possible,
- The patient's individuality must be respected, and any infringement on said individuality deeply rooted in urgent need,
- The institution's personnel must be well trained, up to date and generally equipped to accomplish the tasks they are set,

- No person must be exposed to unnecessary dangers while at the institution,
- The administration of the institution must be able to ensure that its policies are carried out and that it can document that this is so, and
- The institution must make the best use of the available resources and be able to document that this is so.

This reference frame implies an organizational structure which diverges very significantly from the traditional health care system of Northern Europe. In spite of this, although diverse groups have debated these targets critically, no significant changes have been necessary. Both in the literature and in a number of health policy workshops conducted by the author, the reference frame, be it implied or formulated directly, remains remarkably constant. It is therefore not expected that this reference frame would be significantly modified during the planning phase of projects. On the other hand, the reference frame would be the basis for the structure of projects, and these guidelines attempt to ensure community participation in the final formulation of the reference frame. The methodology intended for this purpose is described in appendices B and G.

Chapter 5

PLANNING OF PROJECTS AND PROJECTED CONSEQUENCES

The theoretical background and reference frame for these guidelines have now been presented. Much less than half the work in a large scale project is done with the definition of the theory and background, however. Even the most complete protocol would contain elements that lack concurrence with the realities of what actually happens. Keeping this in mind, these guidelines now move into a more practical set of arguments, turning the reference frame on its head, so to speak.

Elements of the reference frame are examined with respect to the consequences which would be likely as a result of implementing a regional or national strategy on this basis. This is presented through a description of the envisaged strategic planning process and possible scenarios of implementing the strategy. To paraphrase the reference frame in what one might call a problem oriented manner, the criticism raised against the present structure of health care delivery maintains:

- that the system function is poorly documented generally, and in terms of quality (more good than harm) specifically,
- that the hospital sector is grossly oversized structurally relative to the primary sector,
- that the dominating referral systems tend to grossly overemphasize hospitalization, and
- that there are serious difficulties in interfacing the various institutions and sectors active in the health area (coordination).

The reference frame implies a number of system strategies which address these problems, but the implied systems are mostly untried or non-existent. This is the reason for adopting a pilot approach, as the existing information would not support a wholesale, head long restructuring of the health care system. Like the Health for All strategy, there is simply too great a gap between the formulated strategy and the present system to create a realistic scenario over the functions of a regional or national system. It is essential to pilot these strategies in the real world of patients, unions, politicians and administrations, and evaluate the impact of these developments in terms of their utilizability on a larger scale.

The reference frame does not specify a project in such detail that an unequivocal design ensues. Pilot projects could be envisaged in a number of different ways and settings. For example, one could apply certain elements of the CQD list to the activities of a hospital clinical department, or implement a strict home care oriented referral plan in a pilot community. Both approaches would offer important information on the viability of the reference frame. The problem with this approach is that the workings of such projects have variable priority among personnel with a thousand other things on their minds. This is not conducive to evaluation, which becomes extremely complex if not undoable in the general confusion of normal functions (because of all the variables one needs to control and often cannot control) and a limited personnel motivation resulting, among other things, from a limited outlook for projects.

It is clear that all of the problems addressed in the reference frame are extremely interdependent. Therefore, a much more powerful evaluation of the appropriateness of the reference frame can be accomplished through a total or near-total commitment. The strategy is generally intended to improve quality while limiting cost. The only foreseeable danger involved would be of a budgetary nature. To limit the risk in this sense, one could limit the project size through the size of the population involved. In this way, almost all aspects of the reference frame can be tested, making it possible to test a number of hypotheses which have lacked a "laboratory" until present. The questions involved are:

- Is it at all within the reach of human endeavour to live up to the quality level specified in the reference frame (or another reference frame with similar goals)?

- Can the implied referral system hold water? (For example, one serious problem would be how to administrate acute and serious injury services.)
- Is it possible to motivate the medical profession for the extended decentralization of services implied (no evidence to date makes this plausible, yet it is extremely desirable)?
- Is community involvement a real or imagined object (current wisdom tends to depict the community as wanting more of everything)?

The answers to these questions are not known: It is such answers that projects as designed are meant to give. Thus, an analysis of the consequences of the pilot system in terms of regional/national system strategy must await the implementation and evaluation of implemented projects. On the other hand, certain parts of the total concept have been set in motion in different settings. Some of the experiences from these settings were described shortly in the introduction, where it was explained that the combination of the Health for All strategy and the HMO concept were central to the theoretical basis of these guidelines. The theoretical basis has a political counterpart, which is the belief, more and more common in developed countries, that health care costs have reached some form of plateau regarding cost/benefit, and that further increases in funding would not be accompanied by reasonable benefits. A health services research branch is emerging which deals with this side of the problem. In some seminal work, Doll (63), looking at long term trends in mortality and the available data on major disease trends, presents some very disturbing evidence that the impact of our health care systems on mortality is minimal. Building on this work and developing a set of criteria for evaluating the impact of medical procedures on specific disease entities, McKinlay, McKinlay and Beaglehole (65) present strong evidence that the overall cost/benefit of our health care systems is highly questionable.

These studies do not, however, supply specific information on where the fat sits on the system. The political consensus in Western Europe seems to be that the fat needs to be cut, but few politicians have the knowledge or the political clout to get specific measures implemented. Contrarily, the politics of the health care system tend to bowl rational arguments over, jacking up costs with the implementation of every new gadget that comes along. This relative weakness on the part of politicians to control the health care systems which they ostensibly are responsible for (this responsibility is of course very different from country to country) has led to the search for measures which can improve the accountability of the health care systems to their political counterparts. This search has led, among other things, to an intense interest in the US HMO concept. The concept is not immediately translatable to the European setting, however, nor are the European public health care concepts immediately translatable to the US context.

Whereas the HMO concept in the USA is a privately funded for profit or not for profit health insurance scheme with no inherent limitations on the size of the organization, the crossing of the Atlantic places some restraints in this regard. When applying the HMO concepts within European management definitions, size limitations follow the administrative units in the regional or national structure. In keeping with the major problems of management in the health care systems described above, it is tempting to limit the size of the administrative unit which would adopt an HMO-like structure so that it is possible for the management to maintain a detailed cognizance of the health profile of the catchment area. Among health care system policymakers, there is some agreement as to the appropriate population base, which is somewhere around 10,000 to 50,000 persons (66). To facilitate clarity in this context, this unit is called a health district. The creation of the health district as an administrative unit would allow the delineation of a population base for which a closely defined financial and professional responsibility can be defined. In most European countries, some or other form of geo-political administration already exists at this level, commonly as a county or city government. These administrative entities commonly have some or other health care related responsibilities, most often the areas of social support in the event of chronic, health related disability. With the qualified exception of Finland and Russia, however, the responsibility for the administration of health care delivery and health system policymaking lies with more centralized authorities.

The central issue in the discussion concerning the HMO in socialized medicine is economic steering or regulation. The concept of economic steering is ubiquitous in countries with very large public sectors. In these countries, where some 30-40% of the GNP is bound up in public works, budgets are given by political bodies at different levels. Methods of steering vary much, but over the last 30 years or so, the concept of "budget steering" has become very widespread. Utilizing this method, different functional units within the public sector are delineated in an organizational structure specified down to the level of the program director, and a budget is given which may not be surpassed under any circumstances. Eventual budget overruns are very sensitive politically and often end with the dismissal of the program director. Programs are tied together in larger budgetary pools which also are fixed, thus describing a system in which any increase in activity in one area must be accompanied by rationalization or cuts in another area.

Through these mechanisms, it has been possible to steer the total outlays of the public sector within acceptable limits, although budget deficits are also common on the national scale. Through budgetary changes, activities can be scaled back or incremented. From the US point of view, this system has achieved impressive results in cost containment. Although economic steering has been quite effective, its power of direction stops more or less at the program level. Within the health care sector, steering mechanisms have largely been the domain of the medical power echelons. The HMO concept has been viewed in this context as a means of extending the power of direction of budgetary mechanisms further down into the system.

In the Danish context, these concepts have seen a certain development at the committee level, but no administrative changes have as yet been effectuated (67,68).

Although there is a world of difference between the administrative aspects of public health care systems and the US health care system, the bottom line is quite similar in both system types, namely priorities, coordination of services and inter-sector cooperation. The attending administrative problems are also remarkably similar, perhaps mainly because of the internationality of the field of medicine. All of the more advanced systems are plagued with the doubtful health impact of an unacceptably large proportion of the activities of the health care systems. It is quite clear that we now are able to do more for the individual patient than the available resources allow, and the question of priorities gains importance as the technologies become ever more advanced.

The advances of medical technology make the reinforcement of steering mechanisms especially acute. Answers need to be found to the pressing question of what the health care system of the future would look like. In the preliminary phase of the project, thought has been taken to maximize the utilizability of the pilot system as a planning instrument. As such, the project would be designed to function within existing budgetary restraints to remain workable as the basis for a system strategy. Three alternative budgeting or financing forms have been considered. These would be discussed very shortly below in order to facilitate the conceptualization of the implications of a successful project period.

A national health system based on the concepts put forth here would necessarily be accompanied by large scale economic/political reforms. These reforms would be necessitated by the financing of the system. The models presented pertain to a national system in which all primary care, and much of

Richard Evan Steele

what is now hospital care, would be organized in a system of health districts covering the whole country. Three general financial models are presented: 1) in which the health districts are financed through their own tax base, 2) in which the health districts are financed through a mixture of their own tax base, the regional tax base and block grants from the national tax base, and 3) in which the health districts are financed through their own and a national tax base without an intervening regional level. For all three models, it may be assumed that the total tax burden for the population as regards health and social services would at worst remain constant, and most likely be reduced.

Under model 1, in which the health districts are financed through their own tax base, the municipality tax would be increased, and the regional tax decreased. Health district administration would be the sole domain of the municipality, though perhaps with an ombudsman function at the regional or national level. Hospital service would either be administrated by municipality unions (as in Finland), by regional authorities (as in Denmark, Sweden and Norway), or by the national government. Based on periodic negotiations, the health districts would fix pricing for hospital services in a prepaid system, paying for excesses on a by case basis, similar to the proposals for "self-governing" hospital financing in the British White Paper (68). Excessive cases, such as haemophiliacs refractive to factor treatment (the list is not long, and well delineable), would be financed either by the region or the national finances.

The obvious advantage of this model is that the financial and political responsibility would be at the same level, and the public would have quick access to regress. The chain of command in the system would be substantially simplified. Because hospitals in this model would have to justify everything that they do under threat of not being able to "market" their services, they would depart from their tendency to grow to the detriment of primary care. This would of course presuppose, as in the pilot project, that the municipalities did not themselves run hospitals. Avoiding this is as simple as mandating that all primary care beds carry a maximum of one day stays under threat of sanctions in longer cases. This model would also encourage a form of competition between municipalities which may be expected to compete with each other in providing the best service at a given tax level, as these municipalities compete presently in the provision of cost/effective social services. The municipality taxes would tend to be raised or lowered more in connection with the cost/effectiveness of the system than on the success of program directors fighting for turf. Complicating this are systems of tax levelling among municipalities and regions through national block grants and regional reimbursements designed to offset geographical and population density differences.

The most obvious disadvantage of this model is that it would entail an extensive political reform, in which the regional councils would forfeit a substantial proportion of their tax base to the district (municipality) level. It must be mentioned in the same breath that the region as a political entity in Scandinavia is a new development largely designed to control and order the hospital development of the 1960's, and that the political power of these bodies is relatively weak. Their continued existence is a matter of constant debate which has grown more intense since the mid 1980's.

Another serious disadvantage is that the administration of all these districts would necessitate a substantial increase in the level of expertise which the municipalities command. This would be a drawn out process taking many years. The weakening of the centralized regional power may also tend to weaken the cost containment efforts in the health care area because of greater difficulties with inter-district cooperation, but on the other hand, any increases based on these developments would be at the discretion of the voting population.

Under model 2 the health districts would be financed through the existing tax system, meaning that their budgets would have to be synthesized from a number of separate budgetary entities. This indeed is in keeping with the general tendency in Scandinavia to seek ways of decentralizing the responsibility for primary care, but is significantly more far reaching. Within projects developed under these guidelines, the health district also finances the budgets for hospital care. This would necessitate negotiations on hospital capacity much like under model 1.

The most obvious advantage of this model is that it can work under the present set of laws and regulations governing political systems. The marriage of different budgetary entities is administratively feasible; indeed the effects of the budgetary steering described above are presently pushing the budgetary process in this direction. The existing administrative manpower would probably be able to meet the challenge of this process without inhuman effort, but administrative inertia would be perhaps more of a problem than under model 1. The problem of central coordination, which would have to be constructed under model 1, is already in place for model 2, although it does not function satisfactorily at present. Also, this model is the one which the most information is available about, and the one under which projects probably would be run.

The disadvantages would be much the same as the problems which the present system faces. Schisms between local and regional priorities lead to much wasted effort and political maneuvering to maintain status quo. With the financial responsibility for the main part of the budget resting centrally, it may be impossible to construct efficient economic incentives to guide the health district administration in the right direction. Attempts to keep such incentives in place would probably tend to bureaucratize the organization. This would tend to increase the lower administrative expertise needs of model 2 relative to model 1. Also, the centralized tax base makes it difficult if not impossible to distribute the effects of savings fairly, so that the incentive to contain costs is weakened.

Under model 3, in which the health districts are financed through their own and a national tax base without an intervening regional level, the regions as political entities would be greatly weakened or perhaps totally abolished. Model 3 is somewhat of a hybrid between models 1 and 2.The tax system would be changed, with some of the responsibilities going to the state and some to the municipality. Running of hospitals would be the domain of the state or perhaps the private sector with the districts negotiating services much as under model 1. Financing of the hospitalization budgets of the health districts would be a national domain, however. This model is similar to the present system in Finland.

Model 3 would have many of the disadvantages of model 2 and many of the advantages of model 1. Removal of the regional level would tend to augment the autonomy of the districts. Much of the double administration that exists both at the national and regional level could be done away with, and administrative manpower could thus be freed for administrative duties at the health district level (this is, however, notoriously difficult to effectuate). Information flow could be better standardized than in a regionalized system and results therefore more readily available for evaluation. The connection between policymaking and decision making would be strengthened.

On the negative side, it may be expected that the budgetary system would be even more complex than under model 2, and standardization would tend to diminish the districts' responsiveness to local conditions. Furthermore, central authorities would tend to be less sensitive to local conditions than regional authorities.

The necessity of a budgetary model along the lines of one of those presented here is to be found in the mobilization of resources which the budgeting process aims at. The pricing efforts described above, which would be described in greater detail in chapter 6, are designed to allow the transfer of selected services from the hospital sector to the primary sector. Given the success of the pricing strategy, any of the described models would be inherently feasible, and any combination of these would also be feasible. One could even envisage a mixture of public and private systems, where certain districts opted for private enterprise. The system would become modular, so to speak, and the modules would have great economic autonomy (and responsibility). This is the mechanism whereby the incentive for good business sense in the health care sector arises. It is also a method of mobilizing the structure of the health care system to make it better able to respond to changing circumstances.

In this context, it may make sense to have the hospitals as autonomous administrative units as well, so that survivability would become a factor. For certain services such as elective surgery one could also imagine open market forces in the hospital sector, such that the health districts could have some level of consumer power over the services offered and at what cost. Such competitive forces must not, on the other hand, compromise the equality of access that has become a hallmark of public health care systems, although the mechanisms by which equality of access in a competitive environment can be maintained have not been defined. The lure of competitive forces is strong in public health care systems, however, because they are seen as a mechanism whereby freedom of choice for the individual is maximized. This is not addressed further in these guidelines, but the manpower arrangements within the district do seek to maximize individual choice within broad restraints.

Whatever the financing method for the health care system, the budget of the health districts is expected to be the same. The budgetary system for the health district is the mechanism which establishes an incentive to hold hospitalization down to a minimum. As mentioned under the discussion of the general financing models, the districts would negotiate with the hospital authorities on what could be called the hospital's basis budget. This amount would cover the hospital's cost of keeping emergency and acute readiness and ancillary functions as well as a negotiated proportion of the expected hospitalizations for the budgetary period. The amount would be paid out of the health district budget. Only the resources that are allocated to hospital care become bound, whereas the resources that are not hospital bound are in principle free. A large proportion of these resources would be bound to customary services, but part of the resources would be truly mobilized, i.e. the resources equal to the amount which can be saved from reduced hospitalization levels because of cheaper home and community services. This would become increasingly clear as the budget process is explained in detail.

The overall effect of these two mechanisms, to reduce hospital capacity and the level of hospitalization, would be to move services closer to the patient. This would improve the knowledge of the professional staff of the problems faced by their patients, improve the knowledge of the patients of the capabilities of the health care system, increase the incentive for prevention and increase the direct relevance of the service targeting. In short, these incentives are expected to be central in moving the system towards the stated goals.

Chapter 6

BUDGETING PROJECTS

The budget for pilot projects would be the sum total of the cost of all health and social services for the district's population.

A number of methodological problems exist which may make this very difficult. For one thing, it has not to the author's knowledge ever been tried before. There are also definitional problems. These would be solved either by consensus (workshops) and/or publicly debated administrative decision (see appendix G). The district as such (definition of the target population) would fall into the latter category, the delineation of what constitutes a health service would fall into the former. Whatever the outcome of these definitional processes, some of the figures for the cost of the defined services would have been delineated by the time the pilot system goes on line, others would not. The latter would have to be approximated on the basis of available data. The following budget scenario is based solely on Danish conditions, but the basis for the synthesis is reasonably generalizable.

Concerning hospitalization, complete data is available concerning time of hospitalization, patient origin, main diagnosis and major treatments. Data is not available concerning outpatient visits except on a very limited basis. However, systems are being developed which may lead to usable data before implementation of projects. Total figures are of course available at the hospital level, and in a number of cases also at the level of the individual ward. On an experimental basis, some figures have also been contrived based on a system resembling diagnosis related groups. At any rate, it should be possible to estimate the budgetary data for municipalities. Correcting for any significant morbidity and utilization differences, the hospital based portion of projects could be approximated by using the municipality population as the numerator and the regional population as the denominator, and then applying the ensuing proportion to the regional hospital budget. The hospital budget process would be preceded by a pilot study comparing the morbidity and hospitalization utilization patterns of three different municipalities, one urban, one semi urban and one rural, in order to ascertain the necessity of correcting for socio-demographic differences in the budgetary process. Two Danish studies attempting this have produced data on significant differences between municipalities, but they were not carried out with an imminent reorganization in mind and cannot therefore be used as the basis for this process (70,71).

A service pattern adjustment must be made on the figures coming out of the above process. Some of the resources would remain within the hospital budget, and others would be transferred to the project. This process would be fraught with uncertainty, as no figures exist for isolated procedures, and these would have to be approximated. Some figures exist in English, German and especially American systems, and with great caution and careful adjustment some of these may be usable. Otherwise, the figures for specific procedures would have to be approximated using data on the activities of the ward where the specific procedure is carried out and the best man's best judgment approach. This particular process constitutes a serious weakness in the financial basis for projects. It can be hoped that work carried out concerning pricing procedures for hospital functions can be used before projects go on line. Even without this, one must keep in mind that there is no real danger in this weakness, as any excesses to one side or the other would be correctable.

The hospital based portion of the budget would be the most sensitive of the budgeting processes, in that it is out of the hospital budget that the mobilized resources must come. Besides that, however, there remains the budgeting of non-hospital based health care. Data is available concerning the use of specific procedures at the general practitioner and dentist level, priced on a fee for service basis. The budgeting for these two areas is thus merely a matter of collating data. The availability of this data is different from country to country, and there may be problems of access. Over and above these primary activities, the budgeting must include the community and home care activities. The resource level would be based of previous levels of use. The following list may be modified in the final protocol:

- Maternal and child consultations and programs
- Post-hospital training and rehabilitation
- Home care and home nursing
- Home improvements (nursing equipment)
- Food for the sick and disabled program

- Social support for the chronically ill
- welfare
- Social support for acute financial loss due to illness
- Social support for medicine and special treatment
- Protected housing and nursing homes
- Special institutions for the disabled and retarded

The inclusion of these elements in the project budget constitutes the mechanism another major incentive. For example, including social support for acute financial loss due to illness means that the moment the project personnel find a method for getting a patient back to work earlier after treatment than before, the resources thus mobilized are immediately available for other activities, and the moment a patient comes back because e.g. post-operative rehabilitation was not successful, resources must be taken from other activities. Similarly, modern communications systems allow for telemedicine (mobile broadband), so that intense observation in the home becomes possible. This requires resources, but they are modest compared to the benefit conferred. This mobility would tend to maximize the motivation of the personnel to implement the lowest effective level of care while at the same time maximizing the quality of care. Partly because of the limited size of the operation and partly because of the inbuilt mobility of resources, any slack in either resource overuse or quality control would be quickly attended to. The functioning of this mechanism presupposes, but also is intended to strengthen high personnel motivation. This is in some ways equivalent to the motivation of personnel inherent in the staff model HMO, but without the incentive to make profits or increase market share. The workability of this mechanism must await trials, but preliminary contacts with the professional organizations have been very positive.

A problem arises at this point, in that not all services under the headings given above are health related. The accounting system of the municipalities have not been designed to reflect this distinction. For some of the entries there would be no need for segregation, but in other cases the need would be urgent. For social support for acute financial loss due to illness, for example, only a very small part of the total amount paid to the population under this heading falls into the illness category, the rest being triggered by social situations. The account entries are not itemized according to situation, either. A possible method would be to take a random sample of the cases handled by the social welfare office under such situations, evaluate to what extent each case is or is not (true/false/proportion) conditioned by illness, get the proportion from the random sample and apply this to the total for amount paid out under the relevant stipulation. This is very primitive and would only give a gross estimate of the real amount, but as we are dealing with a grey zone anyway (the borderline between illness and social depravity), the problem probably does not have any rigorous solution.

Over and above the budget which would be constructed in the manner described, a number of other economic factors would be included in the ongoing evaluation of the health impact of the project. Some of these would have budgetary implications and others would not. For example, the increase in worker productivity attained by employers because of quick recovery is a factor which would not have economic implications for the project directly, but would have implications for the municipality at large and thereby the project indirectly. Satisfactory impact of preventive interventions, on the other hand, would have direct implications for the resource management of the project.

Many of the processes described in the budgeting exercise described above have not been tried before. It is therefore deemed appropriate that a pilot budget should be devised as a separate project before the budget for the pilot municipality is constructed.

Chapter 7

PLANNING THE FUNCTIONS OF CHC PROJECTS

The budget of the project is the foundation upon which all else must rest, and it is therefore given special prominence in these guidelines. However, the budget would not make the project any more than wealth would make a marriage, and a number of other processes must precede the implementation phase. In this chapter, only an overview is given. More details of the described planning processes are given in the appendices. It must be kept in mind that most of these processes are not considered as finite processes, but ongoing processes that all are in one or more ways essential for the continued functioning of projects. The same processes are envisioned as elements of the corporate leadership function for the health system in general.

One of the central themes in the referral plan under these guidelines is that the project does not run its own hospital. The rationale behind this strategy is that by deinstitutionalizing illness, the project would be able to draw on resources of the individual and his/her social network which are subdued or directly inhibited in the hospital setting. This is a rather nebulous resource mass which most likely would defy measurement by any other than very indirect methods. In keeping with this theme, the referral plan for the project would not be based on strictly objective criteria, but rather put together by a series of workshops. It is imperative that the conceived referral plan is workable and acceptable in that it would be necessary to adhere to it rather strictly in order for the budget to hold. Therefore, the participants in the workshops would be selected on the basis of their authority, activating potential and/or representativeness. The workshop series is described in some detail in appendix B. In brief, the workshops would produce plans for which patient categories would be taken care of within the district functions, and which would continue to need hospitalization. The first of these workshops would be asked to find 40% of the present level of medical bed days and 25% of the present level of surgical bed days which can be removed to the district functions. The subsequent workshops would create leadership and personnel plans and models based on the first workshop.

The referral plan for the district would have a number of consequences for the hospital or hospitals normally receiving patients from the area, and close coordination with the hospital authority would therefore be essential. This is given in the context of these guidelines, in that it is assumed that the same district health authority which is running the project itself also has the referral pattern authority. In an area where there are more than one and perhaps competing hospitals, this coordination would become very complex, indeed.

Other planning areas which need attention before the project can go on line include:

- The political steering of the project. The concept has up to this point pointed towards some form of health committee for the municipality where the project shall run which transcends the regional and municipality councils and includes community elements not dependent on either (see appendix C for details).
- An overview of the manpower needs for the project and qualification profiles for each category (see appendix D).
- An overview of the technologies expected to be used. In these guidelines, the concept of extended home care would be a central issue. It may be expected that the innovative nature of the project would attract ideas for technological innovations, and this may well implicate projects within the project with attending planning and outside funding. By outside funding is meant outside of the planned budget, this could mean funding from regional experimentation funds as well as national or private sources. Quality oriented service registration is, on the other hand, a central issue of the planning process of the project and an outline of the planned system is presented in appendix E.

Chapter 8

PROJECTED OPERATION OF THE CHC DISTRICT

The work done this far in the planning process has led to the description of the strategy for pilot systems as described above. In a number of health policy workshops run by the author and dealing with this area, the work has gone beyond the strategic level, going into some of the details of system functions. In fact, a function description of this nature was the impetus which started the planning process, and the other planning facets have rather been adapted to the function plan than the other way around.

The following description of such a scenario, although perhaps not wholly relevant outside of the north western European context, is designed to give the reader a feeling for the context of the strategy at the local level. Attendant to this description is a manpower overview, an organizational overview and a technology overview.

Broadly speaking, the district would have those functions which are included in general practice and home and community care extended to include advanced home care or the home hospital, if one would. Central to this function description is an institution which would coordinate these activities which hereafter would be termed the health centre (in the US context, clinic would perhaps be more appropriate). In order to carry out its functions, the centre would have acute and emergency services with 10-12 beds for 24 hour use and ambulatory services, social welfare services, health education and preventive medicine, outward going social network services and community support functions, and educational and research functions. In short, a centre which provides all of the needed health and social services in the community with the exception of specialized treatment and care. In other words, the hospital would be reserved for seriously ill patients needing intensive and specialized care.

One major force that would improve upon current conditions is that the amalgamation of health and social services would do away with the cultural clash between the health sector, whose opening time is 24/7 and the social sector, which is normally weekdays 9-5.

The following schematic function description provides a sketch of the level of the services, which would be provided by the health centre and the primary sector for a population of 10,000:

EMERGENCY FUNCTIONS

- Emergency ward, where minor surgery is performed and acute medical help is given, including emergencies such as uncomplicated myocardial infarctions, asthma attacks, etc.
- 10-12 beds for 24 hour use only, meaning that patients which cannot be discharged, either to home care or other community service, would be admitted to hospital. It is essential to ensure that these short term beds do not become a mini hospital. Mechanisms other than a time limit could perhaps be envisaged. Modern capacity for oxygen and suction as well as vital function monitoring in all beds.
- Clearing of more serious cases, transport to hospital and escorting of unconscious patients, etc.

TREATMENT, PREVENTION AND CARE

- Sexual counseling, pregnancy counseling, maternity preparation and maternity self-help groups, obstetrical function for uncomplicated pregnancies (midwife assisted home birthing).
- Identification of risk groups, e.g. complicated pregnancies, pathological newborn conditions, weakened social groups (drug misuse etc.), children's check-ups, and school health programs, health threatening working conditions, dangerous traffic conditions, etc. for use in the planning of preventive practices.

EDUCATIONAL AND CAREER COUNSELLING

Medical treatment including all cases which can be cared for in the primary setting, meaning that e.g. patients with pneumonia, gastro intestinal distress or endocrinology disturbances would no longer normally be hospitalized. This implies a well-coordinated system of home care and institutions for the aged/debilitated.

- Minor acute and elective surgery possible with local anaesthesia, e.g. hernias, sterilisations, lipoma removal, etc.
- District psychiatric services, including group living arrangements, self-help groups etc.
- Rehabilitation, both in connection with local treatment, after hospital discharge and in the home care setting, including inter-professional treatment of psycho-social cases of work disability.
- Coordination of help for the aged, including administration of nursing homes, social network initiatives and visitation for centralized services.
- Administration of technical appliances for home care, etc.
- Health education in the community

Support functions for other institutions:

- Medical support and staffing of nursing homes, etc.
- Support and substitution for general practitioners, dentists etc. in the event that these continue to exist as liberal entities.
- Community activity centre, where the health centre would assist with health educational activities.
- Work force health services, coordination of broader activities.
- Social welfare office, coordination of common areas of activity.

Working relations with other institutions:

- Central laboratory, blood bank, microbiology laboratory, etc.
- Central hospital (personnel rotation, case review, etc.)
- Day care institutions, etc. (preventive services).
- Alternative living quarters (district psychiatry, etc.)

In the following section, the personnel requirements needed to carry out the listed functions for the projected target population of approximately 10,000 are given. The list is not complete, nor, to the author's knowledge, has any personnel cross section of this type been tried in practice, even though most of the elements have been put together in Finnish and Swedish health centres. In all, the list includes some 35-50 persons in the centre itself, and home care staff upwards of 50 persons as well. In the listing, these figures appear together as centre staff, and it is likely that such staff also would have extended exchange of activities, rotations, etc.

- Medical staff sufficient to cover a 24 hour duty system, probably minimum 6. Besides the normal staff, a number of specialists with consultations at the centre would be available, perhaps also including specialized elective surgery of the type not needing complex support systems (e.g. cataracts, arthroscopic surgery, etc.) In all, probably about 10 MDs.
- Nursing staff depending on the need, including nursing staff in the home care setting with rotations etc., on the order of 20-25 nurses.
- Nurses assistants, including home care staff, 40-50 persons.
- Midwives, perhaps one maternity clinic for 2-3 districts, 24 hour coverage. In the pilot project, this function would most likely be left in the hospital regimen.
- Therapists (ergo , physio , psycho , relaxation,etc.), (10-13)
- Dentists (2-3)
- Laboratory assistant/environmental technician (2 -3)
- Pharmacist(s), on call function? (1–2)
- Social workers (12-15)
- Public relations/health education worker, perhaps a specially trained nurse/therapist
- Technical staff (secretaries, building upkeep, etc.) (6-8)

Besides needing specially trained personnel in order to carry out the functions described, the personnel would have to keep up special skills as well as keep in touch with developments in the hospital sector. This situation diverges from the present situation, and training of personnel also needs special attention. The health centre would need to coordinate educational activities closely with undergraduate training institutions in order to develop skills and problem solving abilities relevant in the health centre context. This does not necessarily mean that personnel in the health centres should have a different and certainly not lesser education than their peers in the hospital sector. Contrarily, health science educational institutions are generally in need of a stronger community orientation, which in itself would imply training in most of the skills and problem solving abilities needed in the health centre setting.

Meanwhile, postgraduate training would mainly be the responsibility of the health district. One major problem in this connection would be the maintenance of personnel qualifications and retention of specially trained personnel in an open employment environment. This education must be planned with care and be accompanied by a comprehensive system of incentives which both make the centre attractive for well trained personnel and make centre trained personnel well qualified in other settings. One element in this strategy could for example be to arrange regular hospital/health centre exchanges, such as is practiced in Norway (personal communication). Under this scheme, centre practicing physicians must do three months of hospital service every five years in order to maintain their community medicine license entitling them to a substantial wage incentive. Incentives other than economic ones have also seen use in other settings. Through library services and research facilities, certain institutions have been able to hold a high level of personnel expertise despite significant geographical disadvantages, as in Umeaa in northern Sweden or Tromsoe in northern Norway (personal communication). A high level of staff involvement in policy issues is also expected to hold personnel motivation up through peer review activities and other forms of formative and supportive evaluation.

Besides the continued training of personnel, considerable health educational activities would be integrated into running projects. This would necessitate considerable training for personnel as well as general information in the community (see also appendices D and G).

Project administration would need special attention as well. It would not do to have the project administered by a "stick in the mud". Administration of the project would demand considerable communicative and negotiating skills which are only common among innovative administrators. The innovative and experienced administrator in the health care field is not common, and it is imperative to find the right individual (see appendix B and D). Meanwhile, the organizational structure for project administration is expected to follow the latest developments in administrative structures for hospitals, with an executive administrator flanked by a medical director and a nursing executive, both with clinical duties beside their administrative ones.

Under this administrative level, there should be no official levels or chains of command, everyone else being situated in a flat organizational structure. This is deemed as being a necessary element in promoting inter-professional cooperation. It is to be expected, however, that certain problem solving functions would require the establishment of ad hoc groups, which then would be dissuaded from becoming institutionalized. This is to accentuate the central theme of the project, that of the breaking down of barriers (coordination).

It is necessary to have a clear enough mandate for the project to run quite autonomously. In appendix C, however, a political structure to oversee the project is proposed. The function of this structure relative to the daily administration of the project is left open to the implementation process. This process is in itself an element of the community involvement process outlined in appendix G. Both of these processes should be planned so as to maximize the level of community involvement as an element in the development of the self-care concept central to the reference frame.

Over and above the computer system necessary for the running of the database system described in above and in appendix E, various other technical equipment is necessitated by the function description. These include telemetric systems for monitoring of cardiac patients (Holter monitors and vital signs monitors, both of which need serious up-tooling to modern mobile broadband technology), etc., a compact, portable digital X ray and ultrasound unit in the emergency ward, portable respirators and basic laboratory apparatus (blood gasses, haemoglobin, electrolytes, etc.). Other technologies may become available before project implementation, e.g. CT scanning equipment at affordable prices. As mentioned above, it is probable that projects would attract experimental technologies. Home care technologies are especially relevant in this context.

These guidelines are of course only a template, so to speak, that are designed to ignite the motivation to achieve optimal CHC. It must be kept mind that this functional overview is not final, and that even the final version of the protocol would be ever open to new input from the project community and personnel. Sudden and disruptive changes are of course to be avoided, however, and care must therefore be taken to make the protocol as community responsive as possible before projects go on line.

Chapter 9

ALTERNATIVE LIMITED IMPLEMENTATION

The purpose of creating these guidelines is of course to facilitate planning of pilot systems. The implementation of projects need political support, however, and there is a remote but real possibility that the political will to implement the project would fall through in the end. Therefore, efforts have been and would be made to maximize the usefulness of the information generated by the planning process within the framework of the present health care system.

One facet of this effort is to ensure that many of the planned processes can go on line as stand-alone modules. The incentive mechanisms as such would probably not be effective without including all sectors in the project. However, it is likely that quite good results can be obtained by implementation of some elements of these mechanisms. For example, the quality vectors in the service database system (appendix E) could be implemented by themselves in existing databases, and the information generated hereby would give valuable feedback to existing service patterns. The idea of the capitated budget could be implemented for medicine use alone, facilitating development of physician behaviour changes. Community involvement workshops could be run for general practice, facilitating positive effects on utilization patterns and self-care activities. The analysis of the relative cost of different activities needed for their removal from the hospital sector may be used for rationalization purposes. The post graduate educational activities could be used as motivating systems.

It would be difficult and, relative to the impact, costly to evaluate these activities in isolation, however, and the evaluation is likely to suffer on those grounds. That presents only that problem that the processes would simply continue as they have done in their sub-optimal, plodding fashion.

Chapter 10

EVALUATION OF CHC PROJECTS

During the implementation process and the ensuing on line project period, an evaluation of the impact and the policy consequences of projects would give important information on the efficacy of this type of health services delivery. This would be the basis on which to decide whether more widespread developments of this type should be attempted. This evaluation theme has been touched on in a number of places above and will be expanded below. This section deals with these problems from a different angle, outlining the indicators and methods which would be used in order to ascertain whether the project has any measurable health impact relative to the status quo.

Although the health impact evaluation perhaps commands the most universal interest, and indeed is the primary purpose of the whole process, evaluation of the economic impact of the project is certainly not to be forgotten. As has been maintained both in the introduction and under the discussion of the budgetary process, a significant portion of the budget for health care for the project target population would be mobilized under the project process and made available for alternative uses. A major portion of these mobilized resources would necessarily be devoted to home care and other alternatives to hospital care, and one central aspect of the economical evaluation of the project would be whether this new resource utilization is as effective as the old. The hypothesis is that it would prove to be approximately 25% more effective in cost/utility terms. Another central issue is whether the numbers of personnel needed to care for those patients who are normally hospitalized now are sufficient to deal with the same health care problems within home care and extended community services settings. The hypothesis is that the present levels are more than adequate, although the degree of this surplus is not conjectured upon. Within the confines of the project itself, it is intended to offer all implicated personnel a guarantee of employment such that any surplus personnel would be utilized in other projects. Preventive interventions in the community and the project evaluation, research and development are typical examples of what these persons could be doing.

The project design implies the use of a significant number of man hours for registration and evaluative purposes. This form of evaluative and registration activity is an essential part of the rational running of any health care institution and is one of the basic premises for these guidelines. As described above, it is expected that a significant number of man hours would be freed by the de-hospitalization of health services. The hypothesis is that the extra burden on placed on project personnel due to the registration and evaluative activities would be compensated by the surplus produced by the de-hospitalization process.

Another area in which there are possible cost containment yields is in the area of self-care and the concept behind the objective "The health system must make its position clear to the public, so that the public expectations and the capabilities of the system concur as much as possible." The evaluation of this statement in the daily workings of projects would e.g. have to do with the use levels of certain drugs with low causal therapeutic indexes, such as the benzdiazepines, or the number of therapeutic procedures carried out by patients themselves or their immediate families. Another element of concurrence would e.g. be the frequency with which patients seek relevant services at their first contact with the system.

In the following, the proposed evaluation is described. The four main vectors to be evaluated are:

- the health status (including risk factors) of the participating populations before and at different times after the project start, i.e. the health impact of the project
- patient satisfaction
- quality of care and cost effectiveness analysis
- utilization patterns and cost benefit analysis

IMPACT OF THE EVALUATION

In a broad perspective, this study is designed to solidify the case for decentralized, managed health care systems as a viable and desirable alternative to the strong emphasis on hospital care, especially in, but by no means limited to the European health care setting. Earlier studies in this area have made a strong case for experimentation in this area (72-74) but no pilot experimentation has been carried out which could demonstrate the likely impact of a national, socialized system based on all of these principles in concert. The quality of the evaluation is of paramount importance, as falsely optimistic or pessimistic conclusions could have serious implications for policy decisions.

THE EVALUATION THEORY, STRATEGY AND DESIGN

The evaluation should be semi internal, meaning that the evaluation staff and the project staff work closely together in defining the operationalization of the project goals and evaluation questions. A collaborative approach to the evaluation utilizes the intimate knowledge of the workings of the project on the part of the project staff and the relative objectivity maintained by the evaluation staff. This trade-off is a compromise between maximizing the utility of the evaluation while minimizing the threats to the reliability and validity of the evaluation, an approach recommended by Patton (75) and Weiss (76). Within this semi internal approach, a process termed by Segall as decision linked research (77) should be used in order to focus the evaluation questions. Under this process, the objectives to be operationalized are selected by the ultimate decision maker on the basis of the specific decisions for which the information from the evaluation is needed. In other words, the different elements of the evaluation process are prioritized by those needing the information. This approach solidifies the commitment of the project staff for utilizing the evaluation, an effect of what Patton calls the personal factor (78). The practical aspects of this collaboration would be handled both formally and informally through the described administration of the project and use of external consultants as needed.

Data collection in the four major vectors mentioned above: health status, patient satisfaction, quality of care and utilization. Health status and patient satisfaction data would be derived from patient questionnaires, quality of care from patient questionnaires and provider data, and utilization from a centralized database. The data collection methods would be described in more detail under the methodology heading.

The terminology of Campbell and Stanley (79) for reliability and validity has been used during the planning of the evaluation. In this terminology, the design type falls roughly into the category of the non-equivalent control group design. Baseline data for health profile, patient satisfaction, quality of care and utilization from the pre-project period would be collected from project target population and from regional databases which include data on project target populations. The same methods would be used to collect data at the same time from an area of similar socio-demographic and geopolitical characteristics in a neighbouring region. The selection of the areas would be neither random nor blind, yet the participating areas would be clearly delineated and little difference in their "natural development" during the project period would be expected. A randomized trial would be preferable, but this is clearly impracticable in the case of a project with this level of public involvement.

The second round of data would be collected in the months before the project start date (after the project planning period) and in both localities, approximately one year after the baseline data have been collected. This would be done to be able to measure the impact of the planning process itself in the project area, which is projected to entail a great deal of community involvement. A third data collection period should be planned after projects have been on line for approximately 24 months.

STUDY DESIGN OF THE INITIAL EVALUATION

EVENT

BD   PD   SP   EMHCP-->   FD
--O-----(X)--*--O--*-------X-------*---------X---------*--O---* Project

--O-----------*--O--*-------------*--------------------*--O---* Control

0-2 mo.   12-14 mo.   22 mo.   32-34 mo.

TIME

BD=baseline data, PD=prestart data, SP=project start phase, EMHCP→=project in progress, FD=final data in initial evaluation, O=observation, X=intervention, (X)=planning stage with community involvement (a relatively modest but significant intervention)

Projects utilizing these guidelines would not exist in a vacuum, and the general development of health services outside of the project area can be expected to move to a certain extent in the same direction as the projects. This is indeed the case with a number of similar, albeit less extensive decentralization projects which are in progress in various places internationally. Some of the bias thus introduced would be corrected for through the control group, in which no such experimentation is taking place, but some history bias would persist.

The same questionnaires and data gathering techniques would be used in all three data collecting periods. Minor modifications would be allowed when expedient, but these would have to be approved by the review board. Since there would be a number of different people involved in the data collection process and there would likely be some changes in the data collection staff over time, the data collecting methods would have a slight element of inconsistency.

Selection of interviewees from each socio-demographic area is simple random, selecting approximately one of ten persons for the interview rounds, administered by proxy with the parent or legal guardian of children under 16 years of age. The sampling frame is the total population. The selection is done by random person number generation applying relevant guidelines. The person corresponding to the random number is localized through the person registry where such exist. In areas where such does not exist, an alternative method must be devised. This method is preferable over a cohort method so that a representative picture of the whole population can be devised rather than the effects on a specific cohort. This was deemed appropriate because the interventions are intended to improve the general health status of the whole population and not just those who ordinarily contact the health care system.

The questionnaires themselves are also an issue of uncertainty in terms of validity and reliability of the evaluation, because the questionnaires utilized would not have been used before and the possibilities for validity and reliability testing would be somewhat limited (see also a discussion of this issue under the methodology heading).

Since a certain portion of those selected in subsequent interview rounds would have participated in the preceding rounds, there would be some knowledge of the questionnaires and therefore perhaps some skewing of the responses to certain questions. This effect may be complicated further by the fact that the results of these questionnaires would be publicized after each round. None of the interviewers or interviewees would be blinded as to whether the interviewee comes from the project or control area, and this may introduce an element of observer and respondent bias, especially in the patient satisfaction and perception of service quality contexts. In order to counteract this, it would be ensured that an interviewer does not interview the same person twice, and that the interviewer is not aware of the response to the last interview with the interviewee when applicable. Despite these expected weaknesses, the anticipated differences in the measured parameters are sufficiently large to be well documented by the utilized data.

A third and last aspect of the evaluation strategy needs to be addressed before the methodology is presented. It is the expressed purpose of the project to test the primary health care approach for its potential as a regional and national strategy for health care system development. Furthermore, the project is expected to produce a summarized evaluation report suitable for international publication. Although this is not the primary focus of the evaluation, this aspect would be attended to during the formulation of the questions to be answered. One might expect the demands put on the evaluation from the generalizability point of view to conflict with the formative aspects of the evaluation. However, the former tends to focus primarily on the quality of care and utilization issues while the latter tends to focus primarily on the patient satisfaction and health status issues. It is not expected that the overlap would be viewed by the project management or staff as a serious problem.

On the other hand, one of the main objectives of the project is to maintain a health care system responsive to local needs. This would necessarily impart a local character to many aspects of projects which would limit the generalizability of the conclusions. This problem, termed selection treatment interaction, cannot be overcome, but would be partially sidestepped by assessing not only how well the system works according to its goals, but also how well the mechanisms for responding to local needs work. The evaluation of this factor would primarily be based on patient satisfaction improvement concerning accessibility, convenience and acceptability with objective data from central database concerning utilization relevance to primary diagnosis. The latter would be related to health status data to ascertain whether these developments have any connection to reductions in various disease incidences, e.g. upper respiratory tract infections, neuroses or occupational injuries, etc.

Another potential weakness in the generalizability of the system design is the fact that the questionnaires may be relatively well known and the desired outcomes easily guessed. This testing treatment interaction is potentially serious. It can also be expected that the project participants would work harder to be healthy than they would have if they were not in the project. This reactive effect would be difficult to assess in that this same health promotion effect also is a major objective of the project itself. Last but not least, with so many different aspects of the intervention taking place at one time, it is likely that a number of causes and effects would be occurring which neither the evaluative staff nor the project staff have noticed or thought of.

The validity of the conclusions about the project strategy as a more generalizable strategy would be enhanced by the involvement of the planned international review board. Furthermore, the methodologies utilized would to the greatest possible extent be at the state of the art level, described below. This has been assured partly through the review board process and partly through an extensive literature review. The problem remains, however, that language and cultural differences can confound the generalizability even of these "gold standards". It would also be necessary to accommodate certain national methodological preferences, even though this would mean a further departure from validated methods than the mere translation of them from English to the local language would do. The extent to which these factors invalidate the methods is inherently not possible to evaluate before project experience is realized.

METHODOLOGY

The utilization and provider perceptions of quality of care would stem from database sources for the evaluation. The person data would come from the person registries and the rest from the project's central database system. When planning projects, an attempt should be made to develop a state of the art quality oriented management information system (MIS) combined with an electronic patient records system. A workable MIS hardware configuration could e.g. be on a corporate network based on 2 high capacity servers, 30-40 PCs and 80-100 tablet pcs or smartphones which communicate with the system on via mobile broadband. Such a system would be in the form of a text integrated relational database, meaning that given access, any point reference in the system could be related to any other point reference in the system. The target would be for an average access time for two relations of 50 milliseconds, for 10 relations 1.5 to 2.0 seconds. The long term strategy for the development of this database is to reach a level of data transparency that would allow a nearly immediate evaluation of any of the data in the database for use in day to day decision making processes while at the same time maximizing the search ability of the data. The areas which the evaluation would collect data on from this system are listed below:

- Patient person number/unique numeric identifier
- Referral route where applicable
- Type of attending personnel
- Diagnosis and/or reason for contact (ICD 10CM) and graded severity index
- Time used in contact (based on an automatic time count triggered by personnel opening the patient record. Personnel would be instructed to open patient record at all contacts for that purpose. Compliance would need to be ascertained)
- Procedures performed (ICD 10CM)
- Outcomes of each procedure
- Eight point quality parameters for each procedure

This database would not be available for control populations. Also, a quality of care assessment would probably not be carried out for the control population because of cost considerations. This is because the quality indicators currently in use are too weak to make such an assessment meaningful. The quality of care assessment would therefore probably only be made as a development over time in project target populations. Utilization data for control populations would stem partly from the regional hospital MIS, partly from the billing database for the primary care area. As far as utilization is concerned, comparisons would only be made when the data are comparable in nature.

The health status questionnaire would be developed using common elements from a series of health status measures including Activities of Daily Living index (80), the McMaster Health Index Questionnaire (81), the Rand health status measures (82) and the Sickness Impact Profile (83). For language, cultural and research ideological reasons, the latter being due to an already existing health status measure tradition in Denmark (84), it would not be possible to utilize any of these measures as they are. The resulting questionnaire would attempt to cover the following vectors:

- Social network and mental wellbeing
- Physical wellbeing and ability
- Physical dysfunction
- Disease symptoms
- Medication
- Medical risk factors (chronic diseases)

- Surgical risk factors (injuries)
- Socioeconomic status
- Substance abuse

The questionnaire is administered in person or by telephone, and for children under 16 years of age it would be administered by proxy.

The patient satisfaction questionnaire would be developed along similar lines as the health status questionnaire. The major English language input in this connection would be the Rand patient satisfaction questionnaire (85), but also this would not been usable in its original form. As in the case of the health status questionnaire, there are regional and/or national research traditions in this regard. The resulting questionnaire would attempt to cover the following vectors:

- Provider patient communication
- Patient perception of service quality
- Accessibility, availability and acceptability
- Patient perception of health impact of services
- Physical environment (both health center, home care and health educational services)

The reliability of these measures should be tested with inter-rater testing and test/retest procedures. Inter-rater and test/retest reliability from at least 25 trials should be observed. Validity should be tested by administering the Rand health status measure and the sickness impact profile in English to 25 persons also interviewed with the project measures, and the results compared when possible (including only those scales which are roughly equivalent – this is necessary because the instruments were developed in English, and translational issues could be serious). Interviewees for this process should be randomly selected and sorted on the basis of English language proficiency. The validity of this comparison would be difficult to ascertain, but reliability should be acceptable. In addition, comparisons of interview results with family and provider perceptions of the same parameters for the interviewee should be carried out for 50 interviewees.

Chapter 11

COORDINATION AND COLLABORATION

There is no question that projects following these guidelines would be the object of considerable interest from researchers, politicians and trade organizations.

It would be expedient and possible to utilize this situation for the good of the projects, both in terms of the expert feedback that this would generate and in terms of political goodwill.

Not to be forgotten are the various areas of expertise commanded by regional health authorities. Within these institutions, considerable expertise in informatics, financing, management and project planning is available. Also, regional academic institutions command valuable resources, e.g. epidemiologists, toxicologists and specialists in social medicine.

CONCLUSION

There is no doubt that much could be achieved by adhering to the methods described above. It is also clear that it is not easy to achieve the level of ingenuity and developmental courage needed to get pilot projects rolling. This then, is the challenge, if one wishes to achieve comprehensive health care, then get ready, roll up your sleeves and get to work! The health impact is potentially huge, and savings should be achievable under simultaneous improvement of service quality.

REFERENCES

[1]   Conner E, Mullan F. Community oriented primary care: New directions for health services delivery. Washington DC: National Academy Press, 1983.

[2]   Nutting PA, ed. Community oriented primary care: from principle to practice. Washington, DC: Health Resources and Services Administration, Public Health Service, 1987.

[3]   Abramson JH, Community oriented primary care. Strategy, approaches, and practice: A review. *Public Health Rev.* 1988;16:35-98.

[4]   Bonham G, Barber G. Use of health care before and during Citicare. *Med. Care* 1987;25:111.

[5]   Davis K. Primary care for the medically underserved: Public and private financing. Report presented at the 1981 American Health Planning Association and National Association of Community Health Centers Symposium on changing roles in serving the underserved, Leesburg, VA, October 11-13, 1981.

[6]   Himmelstein DU, Wollhandler S. A national health program for the United States: A physicians' proposal. *New Engl. J. Med.* 1989;102:8.

[7]   Marmor TR. Health reform and the Obama administration: reflections in mid-2010. *Health Policy* 2010;6(1):15-21.

[8]   Kark SL. Community oriented primary health care. New York: Appleton-Century-Crofts, 1981.

[9]   Puska P, et al. The community based strategy to prevent coronary heart disease: Conclusions form the ten years of the North Karelia Project. *Ann. Rev. Public Health* 1985;6:147-93.

[10]   Saltman RB. National planning for locally controlled health systems: the Finnish Experience. *J. Health Policy Plan Law* 1988;13(1):27-51.

[11]   Secretary of State for Health (England), Working for patients (white paper and 14 working papers), 1989.

[12]   Enthoven AC. Reflections on the management or the National Health Service: An American looks at incentives to efficiency in health services management in the UK. *The Nuffield Provincial Hospitals Trust*, 1985.

[13]   Enthoven AC. Managed competition: An agenda for action. Health Affairs, Summer, 1988.

[14]   Saltman RB, Van Otter C. Re-vitalizing public health care systems: A proposal for public competition in Sweden. *Health Policy* 1987;7:21-40.

[15]   Targets for Health for All. Copenhagen: WHO-EURO, 1985.

[16]   WHO. Primary health care: Report of the international conference on primary health care, Alma-Ata, USSR, 6-12 Sep 1978. Geneva: WHO, 1978.

[17]   WHO. Executive Board, Formulating strategies for Health for All by the year 2000: guiding principles and essential issues. Geneva: WHO, 1979.

[18]   WHO. Global strategy for health for all by the year 2000. Geneva: WHO, 1981.

[19]   WHO. Executive Board, Development of indicators for monitoring progress towards health for all by the year 2000. Geneva: WHO, 1981.

[20]   WHO. Managerial process for national health development: guiding principles for use in support of strategies for health for all by the year 2000. Geneva: WHO, 1981.

[21]   WHO. Health programme evaluation: guiding principles for its application in the managerial process for national health development. Geneva: WHO, 1981.

[22]   WHO. Plan of action for implementing the global strategy for health for all and index to the health for all series 1-7. Geneva: WHO, 1982.

[23]   WHO. Seventh general programme of work covering the period 1984-89. Geneva: WHO, 1982.

[24]   WHO. Health Services in Europe, 3rd ed. Geneva: WHO EURO, 1981.

[25]   Weiner JP, Ferris D. GP budget holding: Lessons from America. London: Kings Fund Institute, 1990.

[26]   Abel-Smith B. The rise and decline of early HMOs: Some international experiences, *Milbank Quart* 1989;66(4):694-719.

[27]   Nelson JA. The history and spirit of the HMO movement: The early years. *HMO Practice* 1987;1(2):75-85.

[28]   Interstudy. Quarterly report of HMO growth and enrolment, summer, 1988, Excelsior, Minnesota, 1989.

[29]   Fuchs V. The "competition revolution" in health care, *Health Affairs Summer* 1988:5-24.

[30]   Luft HS. How do health maintenance organizations achieve their "savings"? *New Engl. J. Med.*1978;298(24):1336-43.

[31]   Hillman AL. Financial incentives for physicians in HMOs: Is there a conflict of interest? *New Engl. J. Med.*1987;317:1743-8.

[32]   Hillman AL, Pauly MV, Kerstein JJ. How do financial incentives affect physicians' clinical decisions and the financial performance of HMOs? *New Engl. J. Med.*1983;321(2):86-92.

[33]   Ware JE, Brook RH, Rogers WH, et al. Comparison of health outcomes at a health maintenance organisation with those of fee for service. *Lancet* 1986;1:1017-22.

[34]   Weiner JP. Assuring quality of care in HMOs: Past lessons, present challenges and future directions. *J. Group Health Assoc. Am.* 1986;7: 10-27.

[35]   Wouldiamson JW, Cunningham FC, Ward DJ. Quality of health care in HMOs compared to other settings. A literature review and policy analysis, *Department Health Education Welfare* (USA), HMO office, 1979.

[36]   Luft HS. HMOs: Dimensions of performance. New York: Wiley, 1981.

[37]   Clarke F. Hospital at home: The alternative to general hospital admission. London: McMillan, 1984.

[38]   Steele RE, de Leuww E, Carpenter D. A novel and effective treatment modality for medically unexplained symptoms. *J. Pain Manage*, in press.

[39]   Vuori HV. Quality assurance of health services: concepts and methodology. Geneva: WHO EURO, 1982.

[40]   WHO. Quality assurance of health services. Geneva: EUR/ICP/HSR 023, 1988.

[41]   WHO. The principles of quality assurance. Geneva: WHO EURO,94, 1985.

[42]   WHO. European region, targets for health for all. Geneva: WHO, 1985.

[43]   SPRI. Kvalitetssäkring: Attmäta, värderaochutvecklasjukvårdenskvalitet (Measuring, evaluating and developing quality in the Swedish health care system). Stockholm: SPRI, 1987. (Swedish).

[44]   Donabedian A. The quality of care: How can it be assessed? *JAMA* 1988;260:1743-48.
[45]   Goldfield N, Nash DB, eds. Providing quality care: The challenge to clinicians. Philadelphia, PA: American College of Physicians, 1989.
[46]   O'Brien N, Lowe C, Rennebohm H. Quality assurance, a managerial perspective. *Dimensions Health Serv.* 1987;64(4):22-3, 26-8.
[47]   Council on Medical Service. Quality of care. *JAMA* 1986;256(8):1032-4.
[48]   Steele RE. Kvalitetssikringisygehussektoren: En operationel definition (Quality assurance in the hospital sector: An operational definition). Silkeborg, DK: Unpublished, 2010.
[49]   Kemper KJ. Medically inappropriate hospital use in a pediatric population. *New Engl. J. Med.* 1988;318:1033-7.
[50]   Kemper KJ, Forsyth B. Medically unnecessary hospital use in children seropositive for HIV. *JAMA* 1988;260:2538-42.
[51]   Kongstvedt PR. The managed care handbook. Rockville, MD: Aspen, 1989.
[52]   Vibbert S. Utilization review: A report card. *Business Health* 1990;Feb:37-46.
[53]   WHO. The Leningrad paper. Geneva: WHO, *Personal communication,* 1990.
[54]   Boettger SC, et al. LEON gruppens udskrivningskort analyse, Practicus (The LELOC group discharge analysis). *Danish GP Bull* 1985;9(34):72-4. (Danish).
[55]   Funen District Council. Temaplanlægning, bind 4 og 5 (Strategic Planning Rounds). Odense: *Fyn District Council*, 1984. (Danish).
[56]   Bentzen N, Christiansen T, Pedersen KM. Skadebehandling uden for normal dagarbejdstid I, II og III. (Emergency treatment during off-hours, I, II, and III). *UgeskrLaeger* 1984;4:289-96, 1984;10:763-8, 1984;12: 901-6.
[57]   Davis K. Primary Care for the medically underserved: Public and private financing. Report presented at the 1981 American Health Planning Association and National Association of Community Health Centers Symposium on changing roles in serving the underserved, Leesburg, VA, October 11 13, 1981.
[58]   Clarke R. Hospital at home: The alternative to general hospital admission, London: McMillan, 1984.
[59]   Manning WG, Leibowitz A, Goldberg GA, Rogers WH, Newhouse JP. A controlled trial of the effect of a prepaid group practice on the use of services. *New Engl. J. Med.* 1984;310(23):1505-10.
[60]   Luft HS. HMOs: Dimensions of performance. New York: Wiley, 1981.
[61]   Sundhedsministeriet, Regeringensforebyggelsesprogram (The Danish Ministry of Health, Government White Paper on Prevention). Copenhagen: Ministry Health, 1989. (Danish).
[62]   Sundhedsministeriet. Veje til sundhed for alle. (The Danish Ministry of Health. The road to health for all). Copenhagen: Ministry Health, 1989. (Danish).
[63]   WHO. Targets for health for all. Copenhagen: WHO-EURO, 1985.
[64]   Doll R. Major epidemics of the 20th century: from coronary thrombosis to AIDS. *J. R. Statist. Soc.* 1987;150:373-95.
[65]   McKinlay JB, McKinlay SM, Beaglehole R. A review of the evidence concerning the impact of medical measures on recent mortality and morbidity in the United States. *Int. J. Health Serv.* 1989;19(2):181-208.

[66] WHO. The challenge of implementation: District health systems for primary health care. Geneva: WHO/SHS/DH/88.1/Rev 1, 1989.

[67] Pedersen KM. Blokafloenningafpraktiserendelægervurderetudfraamerikanskeerfaringer med Health Maintenance Organizations (Capitation as a reimbursement form evaluated on the basis of American experiences with Health Maintenance Organizations). VejleAmt KM/ge A:HMO.doc, 29 Sep 1988. (Danish).

[68] Amtsrådsforeningen i Danmark, Amterne og lægebetjeningen i den primære sektor: Redegoerelse fra arbejdsgruppe nedsat mellem Amtsrådsforeningen og Sygesikringens Forhandlingsudvalg. (The Danish Regional Councils, The Regional Councils and medical care in the primary sector: Report of the working group convened by the Regional Councils and the National Health Insurance Negotiating Committee), Jan 1989. (Danish).

[69] Secretary of State for Health (England). Working for patients (white paper and 14 working papers), 1989.

[70] Alban A, Hansen EB, Christensen U. Opgaveglidning mellem sygehuse og kommuner (Service redistribution between hospitals and municipalities). Copenhagen: Dansk Sygehus Institut, 1988. (Danish).

[71] Kjeldsen K, Pedersen OH. Primærkommunernes forbrug af sygehusydelser. (Use of hospital services in municipalities). Copenhagen: Sundhedsstyrelsen, 1981. (Danish).

[72] Kekki P. The analysis of relationships between the availability of resources and the use of health services in Finland: A cross sectional study. *Med. Care* 1980;18:1229-40.

[73] Saltman RB. National planning for locally controlled health systems: The Finnish experience. *J. Health Politics Policy Law* 1988;13(1):27-51.

[74] Conner E, Mullan F, eds. Community oriented primary care: New directions for health services delivery. Washington, DC: National Academy Press, 1983.

[75] Patton MQ. Utilization focused evaluation. Beverly Hills, CA: Sage, 1986:196-217.

[76] Weiss CH. Evaluation research: Methods of assessing program effectiveness. Englewood Cliffs, NJ: Prentice Hall, 1972.

[77] Segall A. Decision linked research in health manpower development. PartI: The approach, framework and methods and Part II: First initiative, plan of action. Geneva: WHO DHSH, 1985.

[78] Bonham G, Barber G. Use of health care before and during Citicare. *Med. Care* 1987;25(111):40-58.

[79] Campbell DT, Stanley JC. Experimental and quasi experimental designs for research. Chicago, IL: Rand McNally, 1963.

[80] Katz S, Ford AB, Moskowitz RW, Jaffee MW. Studies of illness in theaged. The index of ADL: A standardized measure of biological and psychosocial function. *JAMA* 1963;185:94.

[81] Chambers LW, et al. The McMaster Health Index Questionnaire. *J.Rheumatol.* 1982;9:780-4.

[82] Stewart AL, Ware JE, Brook RH. Construction and scoring of aggregate functional status indexes, Vol I. Santa Monica, CA, Rand, 1982.

[83] Bergner M, Bobbit RA, Carter WB, Gilson BS. The sickness impact profile: Development and final revision of a health status measure. *Med. Care* 1981;19:787-805.

[84] Rasmussen NC, Groth MV, Bredkjær FR, Madsen M, Kamper Jørgensen F. Health and disease in Denmark 1987. (Danish: Sundhed og sygelighed i Danmark 1987). Copenhagen: DIKE, 1988. (Danish).

[85] Ware JE, Snyder MK, Russel Wright W, Davies AR. Defining and measuring patient satisfaction with medical care. *Evaluat Program Plan* 1983;6:247-63.

[86] Guilbert JJ. Educational handbook for health personnel, revised edition. Geneva: WHO, 1987.

[87] Steele RE. Peer learning in health science education, an alternative didactic method. Geneva: WHO/EDUC/87.190, 1988.

[88] Steele RE. Policy platform on medical education. Silkeborg: IFMSA, 1984.

[89] Smith RC, Lein C, Collins C, Lyles JS, Given B, Dwamena FC, et al. Treating patients with medically unexplained symptoms in primary care. *J. Gen. Intern. Med.* 2003;18(6):478-89.

Chapter 12

PEOPLE WITH A DISABILITY IN MANAGED CARE

*Joav Merrick**

National Institute of Child Health and Human Development,
Jerusalem, Office of the Medical Director, Health Services,
Division for Intellectual and Developmental Disabilities,
Ministry of Social Affairs and Social Services, Jerusalem,
Division of Pediatrics, Hadassah Hebrew University Medical Center,
Mt Scopus Campus, Jerusalem, Israel and Kentucky Children's Hospital,
University of Kentucky, Lexington, KY, US

ABSTRACT

Managed care plans and health maintenance organizations were
introduced in the United States in the 1970s to provide care for members
at reduced costs. Health care is faced with growing caseloads, declining
funding and high cost, which has resulted that many states enroll high-
cost individuals with chronic disabilities in Medicaid managed health and
long-term service plans. They are doing so in an attempt to place program
expenditures on a more sustainable course, while simultaneously
improving the quality and accessibility of services. As there is a risk that

Correspondence: Professor Joav Merrick, MD, MMedSci, DMSc, Medical Director, Health
Services, Division for Intellectual and Developmental Disabilities, Ministry of Social
Affairs and Social Services, POBox 1260, IL-91012 Jerusalem, Israel. E-mail:
jmerrick@zahav.net.il

the population of people with a disability will not get optimal care, the National Council on Disability (NCD) created 20 principle guidelines in order to secure optimal and state of the art health care for people with a disability. The principles are presented here and it is hoped that states will follow these principles to provide optimal and state of the art care for the population of people with a disability.

INTRODUCTION

Managed care plans are health insurance plans that contract with health care providers and medical facilities to provide care for members at a reduced costs. There are several types of managed care plans: Health Maintenance Organizations (HMO) usually only pay for care within the network. You choose a primary care doctor who coordinates most of your care; Preferred Provider Organizations (PPO) usually pay more if you get care within the network, but they still pay a portion if you go outside and Point of Service (POS) plans let you choose between an HMO or a PPO each time you need care.

In the United States National Library of Medicine, the term "managed care" is defines as (1):

> ...intended to reduce unnecessary health care costs through a variety of mechanisms, including: economic incentives for physicians and patients to select less costly forms of care; programs for reviewing the medical necessity of specific services; increased beneficiary cost sharing; controls on inpatient admissions and lengths of stay; the establishment of cost-sharing incentives for outpatient surgery; selective contracting with health care providers; and the intensive management of high-cost health care cases. The programs may be provided in a variety of settings, such as Health Maintenance Organizations and Preferred Provider Organizations

The idea and concept of managed care and HMOs was born by the pediatric neurologist Paul M Ellwood, Jr. (born 16 July 1926), the "father of the health maintenance organization", who worked with children affected by the 1950s polio epidemic. The Sister Kenny Institute, which Ellwood directed, had full beds with polio victims until the vaccine resulted in vacant beds, which was then filled with children with intellectual and developmental disabilities.

As he was doing evening rounds amid crying children, it struck him that they were making decisions for economic reasons (the need to fill hospital beds) that were not in the best interests of patients. His growing conviction that this calculus – putting the interests of health care providers over patient well-being – characterized the American medical system in general, led him to conceive and advocate for alternative approaches that paved the way for the enactment of the Health Maintenance Organization Act of 1973 (2).

As for the general population and the concept of managed care there has been voices both for and against, which is also the case when we come to the issue of health care for people with a disability (3).

NATIONAL COUNCIL ON DISABILITY

National Council on Disability (NCD) is an independent federal agency charged with advising the President of the United States, Congress, and other federal agencies regarding policies, programs, practices and procedures that affect people with disabilities. It was established as a small advisory council within the Department of Education in 1978, transformed into an independent agency in 1984 and charged with reviewing all federal disability programs and policies. In 1986, NCD recommended enactment of an Americans with Disabilities Act and then drafted the first version of the bill that was enacted in 1990.

NCD works by convening stakeholders to acquire timely and relevant input for recommendations and action steps, gathering and analyzing data and other information, engaging and influencing current debates and agendas, identifying and formulating solutions to emerging and long-standing challenges and providing tools to facilitate effective implementation.

SUCCESSFULLY ENROLLING PEOPLE WITH DISABILITIES IN MANAGED CARE PLANS

In 2012 the National Council on Disability published 20 guiding principles for enrolling people with disabilities in managed care programs (4) starting with personal experience and outcomes for persons in community living:

Principle1 (community living)

The central organizing goal of system reform must be to assist individuals with disabilities to live full, healthy, participatory lives in the community. For every American, sound, stable health is essential to living a rich, productive life. Individuals with chronic disabilities are among the primary victims of the nation's fragmented health care delivery system, with its lack of emphasis on health promotion, prevention, early intervention and the provision of a coordinated array of primary and specialty health services. This lack of emphasis, and the frequent denial of health maintenance services, such as, by way of example, maintenance oriented physical therapy for people with physical disabilities, or personal care supports to help independently living people to exercise or prepare healthy meals, is frequently detrimental to the long-term health and successful community living of these individuals. The resulting health decline can not only sabotage community living, employment, and participation, but can allow the development of acute or serious illness resulting in a far greater cost of the system overall.

The focus of both health care and long term supports must be to enable individuals with disabilities to live as independently as possible and to participate fully in community life, both now and throughout their lives. It is essential that enrollees in Medicaid managed care plans receive medical and non-medical supports that promote health and wellness and their capacity to reside as independently as possible in fully integrated community settings rather than in institutions and congregate care facilities.

Principle 2 (personal control)

Managed care systems must be designed to support and implement person-centered practices, consumer choice, and consumer-direction. People with disabilities must be able to control their own lives and choose services and supports consistent with their personal goals and aspirations. Service policies must be person-centered. They must honor the preferences of the person and respect each individual's right to control his or her own life by offering a flexible array of high quality, personalized services and supports from which to choose.

Person-centered practices. Person-centered approaches are designed to assist an individual to plan their life and supports; to increase their personal self-determination, improve their own independence, and support their social inclusion in the community. The provision of health care and long term supports and services must be designed and delivered through a person-centered lens. Health services must be carefully synchronized with long-term supports based on a common set of outcomes spelled out in each participant's person-centered plan. The plan must enable the person to exercise control over activities of daily living and health maintenance functions.

Self-direction. A state's comprehensive managed care plan must offer enrollees with disabilities the option of overseeing their own direct services and supports and controlling their own budgets, consistent with the provisions of a person-centered plan. This option must include the exercise of control over services and supports related to critical life functions, including activities of daily living, health maintenance, community participation, and employment. In addition, individuals choosing to self-direct their services must receive the training and support needed to effectively perform required functions. In order to promote maximum independence, state officials and representatives of managed care organizations should join individuals with disabilities in advocating for amendments to overly restrictive nurse practice laws and regulations. Flexibility in these areas will provide the opportunity for creative approaches to self-directed care, which, when directed by an individual with best knowledge of his or her own needs, can greatly improve health outcomes, and will often be more cost effective over the long term.

Individual choice. A key aim of managed care is to replace high cost services or programs with equally effective lower cost alternatives. The intimate nature of long term supports furnished to people with intensive needs requires the direct involvement of consumers in selecting the individuals to provide the services as well as the services to be delivered. Managed care benefit packages, therefore, must offer people with substantial, chronic disabilities choices among community based services, as well as the providers of such services and the locations where they are offered.

Principle 3 (employment)

For non-elderly adults with disabilities employment is a critical pathway toward independence and community integration. Working age enrollees must receive the supports necessary to secure and retain competitive employment. Competitive employment at prevailing wages not only enhances an individual's sense of self-worth and economic well-being but often results in reductions – sometimes sharp reductions -- in service costs and support needs.

Employees also have opportunities to build relationships that strengthen their social ties with others and enable them to become contributing, valued members of the community. One key policy aim, therefore, must be to broaden employment among people with disabilities by providing the necessary supports both in and out of the workplace and eliminating disincentives in order to enable them to enter or re-enter the work force.

Principle 4 (support for family caregivers)

Families should receive the assistance they need to effectively support and advocate on behalf of people with disabilities. Family members play critical roles in supporting and advocating on behalf of individuals with disabilities. Given government funding constraints and the growing shortage of workers available to provide direct, hands-on supports, the role of family caregivers is likely to expand in the years ahead. It is essential that family members receive the information, counseling, training and support they require to carry out their responsibilities. State policies also should permit family caregivers to be paid for providing services when such remuneration is in the best interest of the individual with disabilities, as well as providing potential cost savings to the taxpaying public, by ensuring better, more efficient care than might be available from an outside provider in that community, and so promoting the health of the individual.

Principle 5 (stakeholder involvement)

States must ensure that key disability stakeholders -- including individuals with disabilities, family members, support agency representatives, and advocates -- are fully engaged in designing, implementing and monitoring the outcomes and effectiveness of Medicaid managed care services and service delivery systems. Active, open and continuous dialogue with all affected parties offers the best prospects for creating and maintaining a service delivery system that meets the needs of people with disabilities. All participants must be confident that the transition to a managed care system will yield better outcomes for people with disabilities. The involvement of disability stakeholders should not end with approval of a state's managed care plan. Instead, stakeholders should participate in monitoring the implementation of the plan and provide feedback on system performance and needed plan modifications on an ongoing basis.

Principle 6 (life-span focus)

The service delivery system must be capable of addressing the diverse needs of all plan enrollees on an individualized basis, including children, adolescents and adults with physical disabilities, intellectual and developmental disabilities, traumatic brain injuries, mental illnesses, substance use disorders, and other types of severe, chronic disabilities. The demographic and need profiles of Medicaid beneficiaries with disabilities are incredibly diverse. The types of services and supports required by an 85 year old widow with advanced Alzheimer's disease are entirely different than those needed by a teenager with significant behavioral and communication challenges caused by autism or another serious neurological disorder. Both individuals may require specialized medical services and prescription medications in combination with ongoing personal assistance. But, the composition and competencies of the team assembled to deliver those services will be radically different in the two instances, as will the types of medical, psychological, pharmacological and social interventions deemed appropriate. A key test of the potential effectiveness of a state's managed care plan, therefore, is the extent to which it includes credible strategies for serving all sub-populations of Medicaid beneficiaries with disabilities who are to be enrolled in the plan. One-size-fits-all approaches will not work.

Principle 7 (assessment)

States should complete a readiness assessment before deciding when and how various sub-groups of people with disabilities should be enrolled in managed care plans. A state's phase-in schedule in turn should be based on the results of this assessment. Existing disability service systems are highly complex, with administrative structures, operational capabilities and financial arrangements varying widely from population group to population group and from state to state.

Creating a unified financing and service delivery system capable of addressing the diverse health and long-term support needs of people with disabilities is an enormously complicated undertaking. Plan components must be designed and implemented with great care if disastrous consequences for the participants are to be avoided.

If a state's goal is to administer Medicaid-funded health services and long-term supports under a single managed care umbrella, state officials must work with disability stakeholders, to assess existing methods of financing and delivering specialized services to covered disability sub-populations (e.g. individuals with physical disabilities, children and adults with intellectual and developmental disabilities, persons with serious and persistent mental illnesses and substance abuse disorders, etc.).

The aim of this assessment should be to pinpoint modifications in existing facilities, programs, services and administrative policies and practices that will have to occur prior to conversion to a managed care format. The results of this assessment should be used in establishing a synchronized implementation schedule.

Consideration should be given to population-based or geographic-based phase-in schedules to ensure that adequate time and attention are devoted to essential implementation activities and compliance with related contractual obligations are carefully monitored by the state.

Principle 8 (provider networks)

The network of providers enrolled by each managed care organization should include those who furnish health care, behavioral health and where applicable, long term supports. The network must encompass both providers of institutional and home and community-based supports. Each network should have sufficient numbers of qualified providers in each specialty area to allow participants to choose among alternatives.

Special attention is needed to ensure that service providers have the capacity and expertise to address the racial and ethnic diversity of the populations being served as well as cultural and linguistic barriers to access. Care also must be taken to establish and maintain adequate provider networks in rural areas of a state, afford people with disabilities a voice in the selection of network providers (possibly through advisory bodies at the state and MCO levels), and provide access to out of network services when necessary to enable enrollees to receive all needed services, including any supports or services identified as promoting community living and long-term health.

Principle 9 (Transition to community based services)

States planning to enroll recipients of long-term services and supports in managed care plans should be required by CMS to include providers of institutional programs as well as providers of home and community-based supports within the plan's scope of services. This requirement should be built into the "terms and conditions" governing waiver approvals. In recognition of the ADA (Americans with Disabilities Act) requirements as interpreted by the US Supreme Court in its Olmstead ruling, states should be required by CMS to detail in their demonstration/waiver requests the steps that will be taken to effectively transition eligible individuals with disabilities from long-term care institutions to home and community-based settings.

Principle 10 (competency and expertise)

The existing reservoir of disability-specific expertise, both within and outside of state government, should be fully engaged in designing service delivery and financing strategies and in performing key roles within the restructured system. State Medicaid officials should draw upon the knowledge and skills of their colleagues in state behavioral health, developmental disabilities, vocational rehabilitation, education, housing, transportation, and other agencies in designing a Medicaid managed care system that builds upon decades of experience in serving various sub-populations of people with disabilities. Moreover, lead responsibility for planning and overseeing the delivery of specialized services and supports to sub-populations should be assigned to these disability-specific agencies. Another key objective of the state's managed care plan should be to expand and improve the effectiveness and efficiency of existing community disability service networks, thereby taking full advantage of the extensive knowledge and experience that exists within private community service agencies.

Principle 11 (operational responsibility and oversight)

Responsibility for day-to-day oversight of the managed care delivery system must be assigned to highly qualified state and federal governmental personnel with the decision-making authority necessary to proactively administer the plan in the public interest.

Managed care should not be viewed as a means by which state policymakers divest themselves of their constitutional and statutory responsibilities for ensuring that recipients of publicly-funded services and supports, as well as the general taxpaying public, are effectively served. State policymakers must ensure that an adequate number of qualified state personnel are in place to monitor the system and hold managed care organizations and their sub-contractors accountable for their performance. It is vitally important that managed care contracts contain clear, unambiguous performance standards, operating guidelines, data reporting requirements, and outcomes expectations so that contractors and sub-contractors can be held to the contract specifications. Such outcomes expectations should include improvement, or at the very least parity, in long-term health of the population served, and steady improvement in transition to community living. A state-of-the-art management information system is essential to effectively administering a managed care system (e.g., maintaining electronic records; tracking incidents; and establishing payment rates) as well as in carrying out many key state monitoring, oversight and enforcement functions.

Principle 12 (continuous innovation)

The federal government and the states should actively promote innovation in long-term services and supports for people with disabilities. The American health care system is undergoing substantial changes as policymakers seek to ensure that all citizens gain access to affordable health care. There is no shortage of proposals to improve the quality and cost-effectiveness of services to Medicare and Medicaid beneficiaries with chronic disabilities. But, most of these proposals focus primarily on improving the organization and delivery of health care services, while giving little or no attention to gaps and discontinuities in the nation's long-term services and supports system. Building a strong, resilient community-based infrastructure to support individuals with disabilities is an essential part of creating a sustainable health care delivery system. To achieve this objective, federal and state policymakers must stimulate and nourish innovative approaches to: (a) improving access to and utilization of generic and government services; (b) forging creative public-private partnerships both within and across service delivery systems; (c) promoting better use of natural and community resources; (d) exploring opportunities to accomplish essential support functions more effectively and economically; and (e) broadening the definition of services and supports to include those services which promote, maintain, and support long-term health and healthy community living, and in so doing to create a healthier population, more economical for all.

Principle 13 (maintenance of effort and reinvesting savings)

CMS should rigorously enforce the ACA "maintenance of effort" provisions in granting health and long-term service reform waivers. The agency should require that any savings achieved through reduced reliance on high-cost institutional care, reductions in unnecessary hospital admissions and improved coordination and delivery of services be used to extend services and supports to unserved and underserved individuals with disabilities.

Tens of thousands of individuals with disabilities across the nation lack access to the high quality health care and long-term supports they need, as evidenced by the long waiting lists for services existing in most jurisdictions across the country. It is imperative, therefore, that savings achieved through improvements in the delivery of services and supports be redirected to assisting individuals who currently are denied access to essential health care and long-term supports. In addition, health reform waiver/demonstration programs should not be used as a means to circumvent the provisions of Section 2001(b) of the ACA, which requires states to maintain Medicaid "eligibility standards, methodologies, and procedures" through 2014 for adult beneficiaries and through 2019 for childhood beneficiaries. Managed care entities must ensure that the acute and long term support needs of individuals with disabilities that were being met by the fee-for-service system continue to be met following the transition to managed care.

Principle 14 (coordination of services and supports)

Within a well-balanced service system, the delivery of primary and specialty health services must be effectively coordinated with any long-term services and supports that an individual might require.

The most appropriate organizational arrangement for coordinating health care and long-term supports will vary according to the needs of the individual as well as the population being served. Managed care enrollees with complex chronic health conditions should be assigned a health care coordinator with specialized knowledge and experience in assisting individuals with disabilities.

The designation of a health care coordinator, however, does not preclude the need for a knowledgeable individual to assist in planning and monitoring an individual's long-term, community-based services and supports. Medical oversight of the treatment process is essential when the need for ongoing social or other supports is a direct consequence of untreated or ineffectively managed chronic health conditions, as often is the case for many elderly and chronically ill individuals. By contrast, the most pressing need among the vast majority of younger individuals with physical, developmental, behavioral and sensory disabilities is for assistance in establishing and maintaining a productive, rewarding life in the community, and access to the services and supports that will enable them to stay healthy. A state's managed care plan, therefore, must include administrative, financing and service delivery arrangements which accommodate the wide ranging service and support needs of distinct segments of the disability population, including both primary and specialty health services and long-term supports. In instances where health care and long-term services and supports are separately financed and administered, written agreements must be in place spelling out the collaborative steps each system will take to ensure that the health care and long-term services and support needs of the individual are synchronized.

Principle 15 (assistive technology and durable medical equipment)

Participants in managed care plans must have access to the durable medical equipment and assistive technology they need to function independently and live in the least restrictive setting.

A state's managed care plan must afford individuals with disabilities access to the durable medical equipment and assistive technology that they require to live the most independent, inclusive, and healthy lives feasible in their community of choice. Covered services must include professional assessments of a beneficiary's need for such equipment as well as set-up, maintenance and user training.

Principle 16 (quality management)

The state must have in place a comprehensive quality management system that not only ensures the health and safety of vulnerable beneficiaries but also measures the effectiveness of services in assisting individuals to achieve personal goals.

A state's quality management system, at a minimum, should address:

- System capabilities. A state's quality management system must be capable of: (a) continuously monitoring the performance of all managed care contractors and subcontractors and ensuring that prompt remedial actions are taken when deficiencies are identified; (b) reporting, tracking, investigating and analyzing incident patterns and trends in order to pinpoint and promptly remediate threats to the health and safety of managed care beneficiaries; (c) assessing the quality of services and supports provided on an individualized basis using valid and reliable clinical and quality of life measures, such as morbidity, mortality, health related incidents and deaths, reduced use of emergency care and high-cost inpatient services, quality of life, and individual and family satisfaction; and (d) preparing and issuing periodic statistical reports on personal outcomes and system performance, analyzing trends and manage quality improvement initiatives.
- Person-centeredness. Monitoring strategies must be developed to ensure that: (a) assessments and plans are person-centered; (b) services are delivered according to the provisions of the plan; (c) services are tailored to achieve outcomes desired by the individual, meet the individual's needs and are modified as his or her needs change; and (d) people with disabilities are free of abuse, neglect, discrimination and exploitation.
- Qualified personnel. A state must retain a sufficient number of qualified personnel to carry out the quality monitoring and enforcement activities spelled out in its Quality management (QM) plan in an efficient and effective manner.
- Information technology. State-of-the-art information management systems should be employed to assist state officials, managed care organizations and individual service providers in monitoring the quality of services and supports provided to managed care beneficiaries.

Principle 17 (civil rights compliance)

All health care services and supports must be furnished in ADA-compliant settings. Managed care enrollees with disabilities must have ready access to all services and sites where Medicaid services are provided. Such sites and services must be in full compliance with the requirements of the Americans with Disabilities Act and the Rehabilitation Act as interpreted by the U.S. Supreme Court in its Olmstead ruling, including physical, cognitive and sensory accessibility standards. In addition, all modes of public transportation used to convey beneficiaries to and from such sites must meet the ADA's transportation accessibility standards. Services must not only be accessible but must also be culturally and linguistically appropriate. Communication, family customs, preferences and relationships must be respected and factored into individual service plans.

Principle 18 (continuity of medical care)

Enrollees should be permitted to retain existing physicians and other health practitioners who are willing to adhere to plan rules and payment schedules. Beneficiaries should be allowed to select a new primary care physician (PCP) at any time they are dissatisfied with their current physician, have a medical specialist serve as their PCP when circumstances warrant, and be afforded periodic opportunities to change managed care plans. Continuity of health care is important, as is the sanctity of the patient-doctor relationship. Consequently, plan participants should be afforded opportunities to retain existing health practitioners whenever possible, switch primary care physicians and health care coordinators when they are dissatisfied, and change managed care plans at periodic intervals.

Principle 19 (due process)

Enrollees with disabilities should be fully informed of their rights and obligations under the plan as well as the steps necessary to access needed services. States should develop and implement an aggressive education and outreach strategy to ensure that all managed care plan enrollees (and potential enrollees) have accessible information concerning the services and supports available under the plan and how they may be accessed. The state's strategy should include enlisting community-based disability organizations in developing and implementing the outreach plan. Accessible multi-media educational materials and training sessions should be geared to the various learning styles and comprehension levels of plan enrollees and such sessions should be held across the state. Managed care plan participants must receive accessible, meaningful and clear notices about programs, services and rights including enrollment rights and options, plan benefits and rules, coverage denial, appeal rights and options, and potential conflicts that may arise from relationships between providers, suppliers and others.

Principle 20 (grievances and appeals)

Grievance and appeal procedures should be established that take into account physical, intellectual, behavioral and sensory barriers to safeguarding individual rights under the provisions of the managed care plan as well as all applicable federal and state statutes.

The plan should include procedures for ensuring the timely resolution of enrollee complaints and mechanisms to ensure that individuals will not be placed in jeopardy while disputes are being resolved. Appeals should comply with all existing Medicaid requirements, except in the case of plans serving dual eligibles when Medicare provisions afford stronger protections to enrollees than Medicaid rules.

DISCUSSION

People with disabilities constitute a significant part of our population. Their health needs impact on primary healthcare services and all secondary healthcare specialities. When compared with the general population, people with a disability experience health inequalities, lower life expectancy and higher level of health needs, which are often unrecognised and unmet. Various documents have been published with the aim of improving quality of life for people with disabilities in for example the United Kingdom (UK). Valuing People (5) from the UK placed emphasis on improving the health of people with intellectual and developmental disabilities, where regular health checks was a recommendation that is found very useful in detecting unmet needs in this population.

In the past, most individuals with for example intellectual and developmental disability died at a young age due to their additional medical problems, congenital malformations and infections, but today an increasing number of these children live into adulthood and we see the first generation of aging people with intellectual disability. This trend has resulted in not only pediatricians, but now also adult physicians involved in the management of this population (6).

Older people with intellectual and developmental disability have the same needs as other older people do, and they are subject to the same age-related impairments and illnesses. Moreover, because many disabled individuals live together with their families, the burden is double because the family members are also aging and with time, will not be able to continue their care-giving. All in all it should be remembered that people with intellectual and developmental disability are entitled to the same health care that is available for the general population as a minimum, but it is know that (7):

- people with intellectual and developmental disability tend to have a higher level of morbidity and often multiple, complex and chronic health problems
- have higher prevalence of certain medical conditions (like for example epilepsy) and also life style related health risks like obesity and on top also low physical activity and fitness
- experience greater barriers to access health care (in surveys they are twice as likely to report unmet health care needs (8))
- are less likely to participate in community preventive medicine programs that the general population are offered

Different countries have developed various models for health care to the population of persons with intellectual disability. In the United Kingdom the Community Learning Disability Team (8) has been implemented, in the Netherlands the realization of a specialist physician for intellectual disability, while most other countries have relied on the mainstream health care system to care for this population.

In the United States health care is faced with growing caseloads, declining federal aid and spiraling health care costs, so that many states are electing to enroll high-cost individuals with chronic disabilities in Medicaid managed health and long-term service plans. They are doing so in an attempt to place program expenditures on a more sustainable course, while simultaneously improving the quality and accessibility of services.

The National Council on Disability (NCD) has recognized that managed care can create a pathway toward higher quality services and more predictable costs, but only if service delivery policies are well designed and effectively implemented and they have therefore created the above 20 principle guidelines in order to secure optimal and state of the art health care for people with a disability.

There is a risk that this population will get sub-standard care or sometimes no care, so it is hoped that states in the United States will follow these principles.

REFERENCES

[1]   MeSH database. Managed care programs. Accessed 2012 Aug 02. URL: http://www.ncbi.nlm.nih.gov/mesh?term=managed%20care

[2]   Wikipedia. Paul M Ellwood, Jr. Accessed 2012 Aug 02. URL: http://en.wikipedia.org/wiki/Paul_M._Ellwood,_Jr.

[3]   Tanenbaum SJ, Hurley RE. Disability and the managed care frenzy: A cautionary note. *Health Affairs* 1995; 14(4):213-9.

[4]   National Council on Disability. Successfully enrolling people with disabilities in managed care plans: Guiding principles. Accessed 2012 Aug 02. URL: http://www.ncd.gov/publications/2012/Feb272012/

[5]   Department of Health. Valuing people: A new strategy for people with learning disability for the 21st century. London: Dept. Health, London, 2001.

[6]   Bricker JT, Omar HA, Merrick J, eds. Adults with childhood illnesses. *Considerations for practice*. Berlin: De Gruyter, 2011.

[7]   NSW Department of Health. Health care in people with intellectual disability. Guidelines for general practitioners. *North Sydney*, NSW: DOH, 2006.

[8]   O'Hara J. Learning disabilities services: Primary care or mental health trust? *Psychiatr Bull* 2000; 24:368-9.

APPENDICES

THE LITERATURE STUDY BEHIND THESE GUIDELINES

This literature study description gives an account of what went into the development of these guidelines. It is not the end of this process, as this would continue throughout the planning process and project implementation. Some references given below are not included in the body of the paper, the reason for this being that these references have had a role in the developmental process, but are not considered essential for the presentation of the positions taken.

The literature on the development of the health district concept as described here comes especially from Finland and England. The results reported in this literature support the position that an upgrading of primary services at the expense of secondary and tertiary services can be accomplished within given budgetary restraints. Furthermore, it is argued that this development leads to overall economic improvement (11,33). Meanwhile, none of this literature documents this concept sufficiently to warrant wholesale policy changes in this direction. The literature is, however, very sparse.

A number of Danish papers have been very useful in their description of the system as it is and the various vagaries therein. Among these are ones that show up to 8 fold differences in the crude hospitalization rate for 75+ year olds within what appears offhand to be a very homogenous system! (55, 56). Another group of papers describes evaluation methods of the present system pointing towards significant reorganization, but not going into details as to what this reorganization might include (54-56,61,62,67,68,71). A third category of papers of a more international character describes some visions concerning this reorganization, most of which fall within the boundaries of these guidelines (29,34,37,38,49). The remaining references concern methodological questions which have been under consideration during the preliminary research phase. The on-going literature search includes the following subject categories:

- The HMO as an administrative model in a public health system and the effects of the incentive systems built into the HMO concept on the demand for health care services,
- Home care versus hospital care as an economic, quality assurance and patient/personnel satisfaction entity, and referral systems in use favouring home care,
- The health district as an administrative entity, and described experience with delineating health care costs in toto for a given, limited population,
- The barrier complex to system innovations, and descriptions of successful strategies to overcome the complex, and
- Health profiles and survey methodologies.

An extensive electronic library search has been carried out in these areas with the expert help of the Danish Hospital Institute's document list and utilizing Scandinavian, European and American databases, librarians and experts. There is thus ensured good coverage of the literature.

PROJECT WORKSHOPS/CONCEPT DEVELOPMENT

Many of the planning issues which projects would be obliged to deal with are new in nature, meaning that there is little or no relevant experience on which to draw in the planning process. There are numerous ways to tackle this situation, but the workshop method has been chosen in this context. The reasons for this are threefold:

- The *de novo* character of many facets of projects based on these guidelines would be difficult to grasp and therefore potentially threatening to a large number of the people who would be working in them. It is therefore necessary to utilize a planning process which maximizes the information to the key players. The workshop method is especially relevant in this context, as the participants not only are maximally informed of the planning process, but are also part and parcel to the responsibility for the planning process,
- The workshop method is extremely time efficient, and the planning work would need such efficiency, and
- The workshop method is a powerful activating tool. The project would be in need of a critical number of active allies, which in the beginning is limited to the decision process. The workshops planned in this context are designed to maximize the activation of the individuals potentially involved in the project.

Six such workshops are outlined below. Four of these deal directly with the referral plan for the project. The last two deal with a general introduction of the project concepts among professionals in the region and the interaction between the health commission and project administrators, respectively. All of these workshops would involve key players in the process of project planning and later implementation, as far as possible. Of the six planned workshops, only the first of the referral plan workshops need have a fixed assignment. The rest would have free reigns to find their own definitions of the problems at hand.

The working methods would be as described by Guilbert (85), Steele (86) and Steele (87). In brief, the work would simulate an intensive task force assignment which must reach a specified result within the time period allotted, in this case approximately three working days. Because of the commitment necessary for good results, the workshops are run as retreats with the costs being carried by the project budget (this would of course necessitate an initial outlay not included in the budgeting process). The work would mainly consist of small group sessions interspersed with plenum presentations during which the consensus of the workshop would be constructed. The only limitations on the working process would be the time restraints and the objectives set out by the project coordinator. The workshop report would be compiled by the workshop facilitator and a rapporteur chosen by the working group. The report would go to the regional health authority and be put to use in the planning process for the project.

The background material for the workshops would be limited to very necessary documents, e.g. the project protocol and the most relevant papers dealing with the issues at hand, but the main resources for the workshop results would be the participants themselves. The titles of the planned workshops are as follows:

- Workshop 1:   The patient centered treatment system: implications for health policy
- Workshop 2:   Referral pattern for the pilot project I: referral plan and budget questions
- Workshop 3:   Referral pattern for the pilot project II: system function description
- Workshop 4:   Leadership development for the pilot project: leadership profiles, personnel leadership and educational policy
- Workshop 5:   Personnel development for the pilot project: personnel profiles, attitudes and qualifications
- Workshop 6:   The health commission and the project administration: competencies and crisis management models

An outline of the workshop goals is given below

WORKSHOP 1: THE PATIENT CENTRED TREATMENT SYSTEM: IMPLICATIONS FOR HEALTH POLICY

The secondary agenda of this workshop is more important than the output. This workshop is intended to present the concepts used in the project protocol to a number of key players in the region where the project is planned. This should be done in the workshop method, however, and the output is expected to be the activation of a number of individuals for participation in the planning process as well as identifying relevant participants for the referral workshops. The objectives of this workshop could be as follows and at the end of the workshop, the participants would be able to:

- Create an operational definition of patient centered treatment, and adapt this definition to the setting in which they work.
- Analyze what aspects of the service procedures they utilize are or are not in accordance with the definition given under objective 1.
- Characterize the obstacles which prohibit the development of patient centered treatment procedures in the setting in which they work.
- Devise a plan for overcoming one or more of the obstacles characterized under objective 3, and characterize what implications, if any, this plan would have for the regional health system strategy.

WORKSHOP 2: REFERRAL PATTERN FOR THE PILOT PROJECT I: REFERRAL PLAN AND BUDGET QUESTIONS

The central assignment for this workshop would be to outline the referral plan necessary to fulfill the point of the reference frame: that hospitals should be reserved for the very ill. In keeping with figures found feasible by several task forces dealing with this issue, the assignment would be to find 40% of the medical and 25% of the surgical bed-days which can be removed to the primary sector. In their deliberations, the participants would be urged to disregard any barriers, real or imagined, between sectors, and consider every single account with any possible health relation within the regional and municipality budgets as possible income sources. The average (crude) hospital bed-day price would be utilized as the basis for comparison. At the end of the workshop, the participants would be able to:

- Create an operational definition of a comprehensive, community oriented health care system.
- Using the definition created under objective 1, outline a referral plan for the target community with the given bed-day targets as minimum figures. The plan must be financially feasible within the given restraints.

WORKSHOP 3: REFERRAL PATTERN FOR THE PILOT PROJECT II: SYSTEM FUNCTION DESCRIPTION

Where referral workshop I outlines the referral plan in strategic terms, referral workshop II would outline the system functions needed to make this strategy work.

The participants in referral workshop II should for the most part be the same participants as in referral workshop I. Referral workshop II would use the same bed-day price as referral workshop I, and would also be urged to disregard any sector barriers and consider all relevant accounts as possible income sources.

At the end of the workshop, the participants would be able to:

- Using the referral outline produced in referral workshop I, outline the function profile for the pilot project with regard to:
- the health centre within the health district,
- home care and home nursing and whatever other institutions the participants find necessary to include or create,
- medical care and services,
- social services and institutions for the disabled and/or elderly,
- ambulance services and acute transportation services both within the project district and to and from the hospital rendering secondary services to the population of the municipality, and
- outline a system of personnel and system incentives to make the function outline created under objective 1 work.

It is likely that this workshop will not be achieved within 3 days, and provision should be made for extension as needed.

WORKSHOP 4: LEADERSHIP DEVELOPMENT FOR THE PILOT PROJECT: LEADERSHIP PROFILES, PERSONNEL LEADERSHIP AND EDUCATIONAL POLICY

The results of referral workshops I and II would give significant input to this workshop, in which the leadership for the district would be characterized and profiled. Administration of the district would demand skills and knowledge of similar systems and a very well developed facilitating ability and crisis management skills. It would be crucial to a project's success that the wrong person is not put in charge of the project. This workshop would clarify and itemize the different facets the kind of leadership needed and outline a possible search process. At the end of the workshop, the participants would be able to:

- Characterize the problems (obstacles) which would be encountered in breaking down the barriers described in referral workshops I and II,
- Outline the leadership qualities necessary to facilitate overcoming these obstacles within the framework of the referral plan, and
- Outline the personnel policy implied by the outline of the obstacle solutions outlined under objective 2.

WORKSHOP 5: PERSONNEL DEVELOPMENT FOR A PILOT PROJECT: PERSONNEL PROFILES, ATTITUDES AND QUALIFICATIONS

Because of the *de novo* nature of a number the functions within the pilot systems and especially because of a number of newly constructed collaborative axes, the personnel profiles needed within the project would not be equivalent to the personnel profiles needed within existing structures. The main objective of this workshop is to characterize these differences and elaborate on the personnel policy outlined in workshop 4. At the end of the workshop, the participants would be able to:

- Within the confines of the referral plan, find examples of how existing personnel profiles would fall short of the skills needed in the project for at least the following three personnel categories: medical, nursing, therapeutic and ancilliary,
- Outline a personnel development strategy which would facilitate the development of the skills listed under objective 1, and
- Describe whatever obstacle complex is prohibiting the development of the defined skills, and outline a strategy for overcoming these obstacles. If time allows, a strategy with a broader scope than the confines of the project would be constructed.

WORKSHOP 6: THE HEALTH COMMISSION AND THE PROJECT ADMINISTRATION: COMPETENCIES AND CRISIS MANAGEMENT MODELS

Nowhere has any commission sat with the responsibility for a modern health care facility with the budget for health and social services *in toto* for a district of this size. Therefore, some thought must be given as to how this can be done most expediently. Even if it were commonplace, it would still be necessary to give thought to how this assignment should be coordinated in that particular district. The best place to work this problem out is in the workshop setting. This workshop would be somewhat different than the five described above, however. Whereas the above workshops would be partly open to probable players in the district and partly open to other parties with some interest in the process, this workshop would have to await the appointment of the health commission (or whatever form of political steering is in the end adopted) and the administrators of the projects. When these appointments are in place, the participants of this workshop would be the appointed individuals and other key players. In the workshop, the health commission and project administrators would define their own roles and their relative competencies. It is not likely that these competencies would be defined beforehand in any more than very broad terms not sufficiently succinct for crisis management and problem solving.

It is to be expected that there would be considerably more problems to be tackled at the policy level than that which is usual for the committees overseeing the present system. On one hand, the dismantlement of sector barriers is likely to cause some disruption, and on the other hand, the health commission would have a closer and more vocal contact with the community than is usual for such committees. Over and above the problem of defining competencies relative to project administration, the health commission would be obliged to find a working method appropriate for sailing in choppy seas. At the end of the workshop, the participants would be able to:

- Find examples where it is likely that there would be conflicts between the local population and the health commission and/or the health commission and the project administration and/or the health commission and the regional assembly,
- Outline the role and appropriate working methods for the health commission and the project administration in attacking these conflicts, and
- Outline a general working method for solving conflicts of interest in the project period, and describe the implications of this outline for the work load, work plan and cost of the health commission's work.

POLITICAL ISSUES AND PROJECT STEERING

In these guidelines, many questions and processes are described which are likely to have significant impact on the local and regional political structures. Indeed, a central issue in the guidelines is health impact, and health impact means societal impact. One clear political issue in this process is decentralization. Decentralization is often used as a tool to increase the local relevance of certain measures, but there is a well-known dichotomy between decentralization and central control. Projects adhering to these guidelines would be sensitive to this dichotomy, and although it well may be that projects are feasible under current political structures, it may also well be that some aspects of the obstacle complex to the realization of the reference frame lie in political structures.

It is beyond the scope of the evaluation of projects to analyze these socio-political issues. On the other hand, the existence of a socio-political climate conducive for projects is essential for their implementation. At the same time, the whole idea that the present systems do not adhere to the wishes and needs of the population necessitates a mechanism whereby community involvement becomes a significant issue (see also appendix G). It is not known to what extent these needs can be met within the existing structures. It is thought to be expedient, however, to create a quasi-political structure which would facilitate both the socio-political climate and the significance of community involvement. One way of approaching this problem would be to create a forum in which the parties involved in the different camps meet and discuss ways of amalgamating their needs.

A number of experiences have made politicians wary of "user commissions", as they have been dubbed. These bodies tend to bypass the democratically elected political steering and lead to double administration. For this reason, the idea of the health commission has met with mixed reactions. It is deemed, however, that the experimental nature of projects started under these guidelines warrant a modified "user commission" approach, despite the potential political fallout. The argument is that only through the health commission approach would it be possible to get enough politician/professional/citizen communication going to make the sector barrier breakdown practicable. In other words, no power group should be left out of the process. This would make it more difficult to fuel a short term reaction into a serious problem.

The Finnish health commissions have been met with considerable critique due to their lack of effectiveness. This could be taken by some as a good argument not to have one. Saltman (5) argues very strongly, however, that the reason for the lack of effectiveness on the part of the Finnish health commissions is the fact that the practical financial competency lies with the central government. In effect, the contact is directly between medical directors and the central government, and the local health commissions are bypassed in important matters. If these commissions were given financial responsibility, meanwhile, it would be expected that they would also gain greater relevance and effectiveness. This is indeed a matter of great concern on the part of Finnish health authorities, and the health commission as a health policy body at the local level is again gaining importance there. This development is thought to be the most expedient way of addressing the lack of coordination between institutionalized and non-institutionalized care that is still plaguing the Finnish system.

In the United States a form of health commission has been in existence for many years in the form of boards of directors for health insurance companies. Although these boards cannot be compared to the foreseen health commission for pilot projects, there are certain parallels between the board of directors for a staff model HMO and the health commission. The differences are perhaps more obvious than the parallels, however. One very important difference is that HMO boards must take market influences into account, in that dissatisfied insurees are free to choose another insurer. In this way, quality incentives are thought to play a significant role in the running of these HMOs' services. These boards have significant policy impact on their organizations, and can be said to have played an important role in the rationalization of health care that some HMO's have been able to achieve.

All of the above strengthens the argument that it would be desirable to create a health commission as a political overseer with budgetary competence and policy responsibility. Below is given a proposal for the composition of such a health commission:

- A member of the regional council (politician)
- A member of the regional health authority (administrator)
- A member of the regional social authority (administrator)
- A member of the municipal council (politician)
- A member of the municipal social office (administrator)
- One surgeon and one internist from the hospital connected with the municipality (professional)
- Two general practitioners from the municipality (professional)
- The nursing director from the hospital connected with the municipality (professional)
- The director of the home nursing unit in the municipality
- Four citizens chosen by the above members of the commission from among applicants incoming after public advertisement
- The project administrator

It would be up to the health commission workshop to decide on the chairmanship, etc., and whether the project administrator would have full or limited membership. It is envisaged that the project staff would function as a secretariat for the health commission.

The idea is that the health commission would have final financial competence within the level set by the financial committees of the region and the municipality. The latter cooperation would be necessitated by the budget process. There would not therefore be any need of further political control, unless one could imagine a joint session of the financial committees of the region and the municipality e.g. on a biyearly basis.

It would be desirable from an administrative point of view to create the health commission at a relatively early stage of the planning process, e.g. six months before the scheduled project start. For the same reason, the project administrator should be retained at the same time, and the health commission workshop should be run at the earliest possible time thereafter. The health commission could then act as a sparring partner in the planning process while the project administrator participated actively in the planning process.

Formal guidelines and regulations need of course to be put in order in this connection, but the intricacies of this process would be left to the lawyers working for the regional council.

PERSONNEL PROFILES AND DEVELOPMENT

Above, the expected personnel cross section for projects is outlined. This cross section would be elaborated upon in referral workshop II. It has also been touched upon in a number of different contexts that many of the functions of the district would diverge in significant ways from the functions carried out in the present healthcare and social systems. The purpose of this appendix is to point out in a little more detail what some of the implications of these differences are for the various personnel categories.

In the reference frame, "The health problem of the patient must be approached in a holistic fashion, which is best accomplished through an inter-professional approach", aims toward an operationalization of the biopsychosocial disease paradigm. The background for this may be found elsewhere (38, 89). Let it suffice to say that despite major advances in medical technologies which have made spectacular come backs from deadly diseases possible, morbidity and mortality are influenced only to a limited degree by these advances. The case for social causes of many disease entities is accepted in most circles, although the proof is difficult if not impossible. Notwithstanding this lack of hard evidence, it is thought that significant advances can be made by treating socially caused illnesses with both medical and social interventions. This is generally not possible within the confines of the present health care systems, among other reasons because of the poor coordination between sectors.

The needed coordination is not created merely by bringing the players into physical juxtaposition. The personnel involved must be sensitized to the issues involved, and there must be incentives to coordinate activities over and above positive attitudes. A major rationale behind the inter-professional team which is expected to man the health district is the bringing together of a professional mix which in itself includes enough opposites in paradigm tradition to keep a reasonable give and take going. Meanwhile, it is probable that a large portion of the lack of activities on the part of health care personnel in service coordination is a function of a lack of knowledge on the part of the same personnel about the potential system impact of this development. That in itself is not expected to be a serious problem in projects, because the recruitment process would be designed to attract especially those professionals who are sensitized to this potential. When and if projects have a serious policy impact on the national health care system, however, this issue would have serious implications for the design of undergraduate training programs for health care personnel. For a more detailed digression on these subjects see Guilbert (86) and Steele (87,88).

In the profile description for the recruitment process, emphasis would be needed on the generalist side of competencies as well as on specific collaborative skills. There would not be sufficient numbers of especially physicians and specialized nurses in order to cover a large number of specialties. Other important characteristics for the project personnel would be evaluative and epidemiological skills, political acumen and creative courage, to name a few.

In traditional health care institutions such as hospitals, cooperation is a matter dealt with in hierarchical structures. This manner of cooperation is not considered adequate for CHC. The development of good cooperative habits would to some extent be dependent on a dynamic administration, but the personnel would need extensive support to make cooperative habits develop and grow. This support can take form in e.g. formal cooperative personnel bodies, but it is envisaged that the cooperative efforts of the district would take on a more problem oriented character. As such, relevant task forces could be created ad hoc and disbanded after their conclusion.

Various research activities are mentioned throughout these guidelines. It is expected that the recruitment process, over and above the already covered competencies, would attract personnel with research skills. This would be necessary in order to ensure that the project personnel understand the need for accurate data and work actively in all aspects of the project's function to maximize the quality of the data. The personnel would also be expected to participate actively in the ongoing evaluation process of the project.

Health education should also be an integral part of the skills profile for all personnel groups in the project. This is in keeping with the point in the reference frame, "the institution must imbibe the patient with sufficient information about their condition in order to facilitate the best possible decision concerning the course of the interventions". This is not a process which would be limited to the population under treatment, but the whole population of the municipality. The personnel would be expected to participate in the planning, implementation and evaluation of community interventions with this goal in mind. In the services, the personnel as the patient's advocate would be developed in keeping with the overall goals of the project.

These few lines are by no means meant as a complete reader on the personnel profiles for pilot projects. This theme would be expanded on considerably during the planned workshop 5: Personnel development for the pilot project: personnel profiles, attitudes and qualifications.

QUALITY ORIENTED SERVICE REGISTRATION

Service registration has for many years been a mark of quality consciousness on the part of health care providers. In patient records, nursing protocols, immunization records etc. a giant wealth of information is stored pertaining to individual services. Information is recorded pertaining to diagnosis, interpretation of patient complaints, objective findings etc. all in a form which can lead to an evaluation of the given treatment, e.g. through peer review. Because of obvious time limitations, however, health care administrators are not able to evaluate system function on a case by case basis. Until now, no form of service registration has been devised which allows an overview to be given on an *ad hoc* basis. With the development of advanced relational database models, however, we are approaching the stage where the main body of information recorded in patient records can be stored in a form which allows more or less free associations for evaluative purposes. Integrity of data always becomes an issue when dealing with this area, but in the case of patient records, the truth is that electronic records would most likely be less accessible to non-authorized persons than the present paper systems, contrary to commonly held attitudes on the subject.

The age of the paperless health care institution is already a reality to a large extent, and there are obvious advantages to having a reasonable body of quality relevant patient data stored electronically. In the context of these guidelines, the basis for planning this facet of the service registration has to do with the overall theme in the quality assurance reference frame: "It must be documentable that each and every intervention conducted by the health system does more good than harm to the patient." It follows that we must register information which can tell us whether this has been accomplished. The extreme implication of this line of thinking is that any service or test that gives a "normal" result should have been omitted. This is especially true of procedures that carry an appreciable risk to the patient or challenge the integrity of the patient, e.g. blood tests. In practice, however, one must accept a certain level of normal tests in order to be reasonably sure to catch all the abnormal cases.

Meanwhile, only a small minority of health service procedures have been through a quality assurance evaluation process. The purpose of the development of a quality oriented service registration is to make quality assurance evaluation possible for a greatly increased number of procedures in an on-going fashion. It is to be expected, as has been experienced in clinical chemistry settings (unpublished results), that the mere fact that physicians are presented with information concerning the inefficient use of a service is a powerful behaviour modifier. This information is simply not available on a large scale from present systems. The question of who shall have access to this body of information is not discussed in detail here, but let it suffice to say that the questions of patient anonymity and professional standards must not be compromised unduly, i.e. data should only be made available to relevant persons. This problem is straightforward (albeit not simple) in an advanced relational database, where both absolute and relative access can be ordered and tracked for all categories of data.

The following is a narrative description of the database structure intended for use with pilot projects. The description is not exhaustive and would be developed further during the planning process for pilot projects. The database structure itself and attendant documentation could also be made available to interested parties. Quality orientation is not an addendum to this structure, but an integral part of it. Obviously, all of the described information would not necessarily be available for all services, as the general patient history would not be collected while treating an in-grown toe nail. In general, however, the patient service database would be supplemented by the health profile database, from which some of the information would be available (see appendix F). For each service rendered the following information would available:

- patient personal data
- time/date
- requesting institution, department
- personal data of requesting agent
- receiver of result
- time of result receipt

- consequence of the result
- impact on the patient's condition (graded and specific)
- causing further investigation (specified)
- caused by other investigations (specified)
- causing referral of patient (destination)
- research activity?
- patient satisfaction
- personnel satisfaction
- patient transport distance
- specialist access (specified)
- community service level before/after
- health profile (see appendix F)

HEALTH PROFILE AND IMPACT STUDY

In later years, a new branch of epidemiology called epidemiology of health services delivery has evolved. The purpose of this science is to elucidate the extent to which the service profiles of health care systems have a measurable impact on the health of the population which they serve. This impact is called "health impact". Health impact is a term which has gained acceptance in a number of areas not directly linked to health care systems, such as industrial pollution. Unfortunately, there is not much conclusive information on the extent to which our present health care systems have any health impact. Few would doubt that they indeed have such an impact, but we are not able to quantitate it or say e.g. that system type A has a greater health impact than system type B. It is hoped that projects developed under these guidelines would offer significant opportunity for bettering this situation, as the project would be followed from its conception and throughout by experts in the field.

Probably the most significant factor in this lack of documentable health impact is the lack of widely accepted indicators of health. Some systems have been put together, and these generally fit under the heading of health profiles. Such profiles seek to encompass the aspects of health reflected in the WHO definition of health, the feeling of "physical, social and mental wellbeing". As such, health profiles seek to measure parameters for these vectors. The methodologically most well developed to date has been done under the Alameda County Study (43), but the methods described here would be too cumbersome as a routine procedure. A recent Danish health profile study demonstrates a less cumbersome method, but unfortunately the analysis of the gathered data is not particularly lucid (62). In other Danish studies, large questionnaires similar to the Alameda County Study questionnaires were utilized (64,65), and also this methodology is too cumbersome for routine use.

Meanwhile, these studies have elucidated some factors which have significance for the design of the health impact evaluation of pilot projects.

- It has become clear that the health care system as we know it is one of the less significant factors influencing the health of populations,
- There is a clear communication gap between health care professionals and patients,
- The level of self-care is significant, with a majority of the conditions that individuals view as disease are treated by household remedies,
- The populations have many diseased conditions that the health care system never comes into contact with,
- The individual's perception of disease is closely related to that individual's feeling of mental wellbeing.

These statements have been translated into a set of 7 vectors which are intended to be a part of the routine registration process within pilot projects. It would not be possible or expedient to gather information on all of these vectors at all contacts. Some of the information would be gathered at patient contacts, some gathered during independent profile studies, and some accessed through central databases for person data. It is not possible to define in detail the exact structure of this data gathering process before projects get going. The seven vectors are:

- Mental wellbeing and social network,
- Physical state and exercise, etc.,
- Nutrition and substances (alcohol, drugs etc.),
- Risk behaviour (social),
- Social status (education, work, economic status),
- Chronic disease and handicaps, and
- Manifest disease

Existing databases concerning these vectors are not presently compatible, nor would this be expedient (or safe, probably) on a national scale. Also, the only vectors with a reasonable coverage data wise are 5 and 7. As an integral part of pilot projects, data sets would be designed which cover all 7 vectors with the greatest possible and acceptable level of detail. Ideally, the data set would be updated in an ongoing fashion, and cross sectional data would then be available at will.

In practice, however, the target would be to have a baseline data set for the target population, a data set after the planning process at the time of the project start and after 2 years of project time.

A decision should be made as to whether to attempt to have a data set for a comparable population which does not go through the described planning and project process.

Although this would be desirable from an epidemiological point of view, the cost/benefit of this comparison is questionable. A factor which should be taken into consideration is the activities in the health profile area which are currently under development in a number of municipalities. The existence of a baseline health profile would weigh heavily on the final choice of a municipality as the target population.

Another factor is that a large number of university students have expressed interest in working with projects under these guidelines. The area of the health profile studies is one of the more obvious areas for collaboration in this sense.

Finally it must be repeated that the health profile work would be an integral part of the daily operation of the health district, and that as such the normal personnel of the district would in the long run be expected to carry out this work as a matter of routine. This is a central aspect of the community based concept; it is the mechanism whereby preventive interventions can be directed to needy areas and their impact thus maximized.

COMMUNITY INVOLVEMENT

It is stated a number of places above that our present systems do not correspond satisfactorily to the wishes and needs of the population. This may sound strange in light of a number of patient satisfaction studies showing satisfaction levels with most facets of the health care systems of around 80% (unpublished data and newspaper and magazine sources). There are, however, many serious methodological problems with the ways in which these figures were reached. The general kind of question asked in the surveys is "Are you generally satisfied with the admission procedure at your hospital?" This is equivalent to asking, "Are you generally satisfied with your car?" The point here is that the satisfaction shown by these sources gives very little if any information on whether the present health care system is as the population wishes and needs it to be. Even taken at face value, these sources tend to show a direct dissatisfaction rate of about 15%, which is quite unacceptable for a public service (the figures do not seem to vary much whether the evaluation is of public or private hospitals).

A different kind of consensus has been evolving as the result of a large number of public meetings, political debates and workshops. In this process, the general working method has been to get the participants in the process to characterize their concept of the ideal health care system. The main body of these characterizations point toward a system built around a primary care organization comprised of a large number of small, local and efficient centres taking care of most of the health care problems and a reduced hospital sector taking care of the seriously ill (35,40,41,45). In other words, something similar to the points in these guidelines. The operationalization of an ideal always involves some compromises, however, and measures must be taken to ensure a reasonable trade-off between the ideal and the rational. The literature relevant in this context has especially pertained to the process of community intervention and the methods for making public health innovations work (4,44). It is not intended to review the literature here, but only to note that the experiences of these and other authors should be taken into account.

The task of community involvement has to do with this issue, but at the same time attends to the much broader issue of self-care and health education. The first line of attack of this process should be the health commission and the workshop especially devoted to the health commission (see Appendix B). One of the intents of that workshop is to throw some light on the method on involving larger numbers of the community in the planning process for the project at large. Some considerations are already available. In the municipalities under consideration, there exist groups at the grass root level dealing with e.g. pregnancy and maternity issues, old age care issues, community activity issues and social network issues. These groups are natural receivers of intervention proposals, but care must be taken not to bowl them over. One way of getting such groups involved is to offer them some simple, limited activity support, e.g. access to a copy machine and computer work station. Another incentive is limited stipends and grants for grass roots projects, which normally can be run on a shoe string budget. A third incentive is access to the decision process as such, which e.g. can be arranged as a series of hearings or invitees to committee work. This process is naturally groping, and it is not expected that patent answers can be found to the question of methodology. Contrarily, the very nature of this form of contact necessitates a lightweight, flexible communication interface. The idea of an activity centre is recurrent in the context of the idealization of the health centre, and this should be accommodated to the fullest practicable extent.

Information to the general community would also be necessary. This should not be left to the devices of the grass roots people, although they certainly can be helpful in this context, e.g. for piloting brochures, etc. An approach with has met with guarded success in the healthy city campaign is a health newspaper on a regular basis, e.g. monthly. Other options could be explored, e.g. local radio and or television channels. The public information campaign is expected to be headed up by a special media worker, perhaps a specially trained nurse or therapist.

Obviously, this facet of the project design is incomplete in these guidelines. It has high priority, but it cannot be planned in detail without a project base. Every effort should be made to bring the issue of community involvement forth as a significant vector in the planning process, and the methods developed as the project planning moves along.

ACKNOWLEDGMENTS

About the Author

My name is Richard Evan (Rick) Steele. My running title is Medical Doctor, Master of Public Health, Postdoctoral Certificate in health services research and Board Certified Specialist in Public Health Medicine. I am a clinical Generalist with a highly tuned nose for where the clinical problem (s) is/are. It is the (s) that is the most critical for patients, and the doctor that can and will give time and space for the whole patient is rare, indeed. I am not highly popular, for this characteristic is time consuming and therefore expensive, and expensive is not popular in administrative circles. I command the full spectrum of what can and especially what cannot be done for patients in nearly all areas of medicine and public health. A good example of the latter category is a patient with terminal cancer disease. The oncologists are rarely attuned to the need for a status regarding the patient's condition, but are rather more attuned to describing the possibilities of aggressive treatment. As a consumer of these patient records, one is often left with a serious lack of position regarding where the patient is in terms of life expectancy. In other words, I am often the doctor that breaks the news to the patient that his or her life expectancy is less than six months, and that continued chemotherapy and/or radiotherapy is likely to cause more harm than good. The curious thing about this is that the average cancer patient in this situation is seriously relieved by this information rather than perceiving it as negative news.

In my youth, I travelled extensively and spent time in places most people only dream about, for example about three months in the jungle of eastern Congo with a tribe of pygmies. These experiences have given me a very different perspective on most things human than most other people. This contributes to my uniqueness. I married my wife 37 years ago and we have three children born in 1981, 1986 and 1988. Typical for my approach to things in general, my approach to the issue of how to handle the question of language with the kids was to research the literature and find the best approach. There were many works on the subject of bilingual language upbringing, but the best was from Sweden. The main problem with bilingual upbringing, it seems, has more to do with the cultural value of language one and language two than any other factor. When the languages are equal in cultural value, such as English and Danish, the best approach was to have one parent, one language. This we practiced, and when the family moved to Baltimore, where I was to study at Johns Hopkins University, the children took up the language and were fluent in English after two or three weeks there.

I started medical school late after amassing quite a bit of life experience. This led to some serious problems with the medical faculty, that had a hard time understanding why this one student could at the same time seem so avid and eager to learn and equally critical of the way medical school was run. The first year of medical school in Denmark at the time was purely theoretical with no patient relevance whatsoever. After a biophysics examination, when the faculty failed 74% of the exams, I helped to lead the sit-in that led to the admonishing of the institute by the Department of Education and a new examination, which led to a passing percentage of 78%. Bureaucrats abound everywhere, and in academic settings not least.

The restrictive atmosphere of the Danish system did not by any means suit my ideology, and I left for Baltimore, namely Johns Hopkins University. This institution is truly amazing. Any question one can think of asking in health or public health, you learn at Hopkins to either find the answer, or find the best expert in the field, or find the list of folks that are most likely to help you, all in the space of 10-15 minutes. Once you learn that, it never leaves you.

Further, I have massive teaching and leadership experience, and a meeting I lead is one that is optimally efficient. In systems where optimal leadership is not appreciated, optimal meeting leadership is neither. One could get the idea that no system would be without such leadership, but in truth, few systems want it. The reason? Tradition and bureaucracy. "We are in shit up to our necks, do not make waves!"

This story could go on and on, but the short end of the long story is that I have floated against all odds in any and every imaginable setting and come out fighting. Fighting especially and increasingly for all of those patients that are marginalized by systems that are tuned to clearly defined patients that have well defined clinical workups and treatment plans. That attitude is prioritized in the thesis here presented, where the issues of the marginalized patient is one of the major motivating factors behind the reason why to do everything better.

What is less clear to the powers that be: this is a story that can be told and retold, and taught to any and all willing to listen. Have tongue, will travel.

ABOUT KLINIKKEN LIVET

Klinikken Livet (KL) is a private clinic conceived out of an enormous need for a flexible, reactive and responsive team effort to treat those conditions that have met only a lack of ability to react to relevant needs and little responsiveness to patient needs, as well insufficient funding and rigid thinking, which does not help these patients. One need only to ask the reader to look around a little – everyone knows at least one and most people know several patients that have been told by the doctors, "Sorry, there is not much we can do for you." KL arose from my experience in social services, where these cases abound. Seeing these cases as a medical advisor with massive clinical and organizational experience with creative thinking, I tried to get the authorities I was working with to arrange for relevant services for these patients. A few authorities were open to this line of thinking, but unwilling to arrange for the services in the public sphere. This led to the opening of the private clinic that engaged myself, psychologists, relaxation therapists, physiotherapists and an ad hoc collection of specialists in various fields as needed, for example a rheumatologist, an X-ray specialist or an occupational advisor.

KL showed that a collaborative effort led by a relevant Generalist (this term is capitalized purposely – this function cannot be carried out by a generalist without relevant public health and organizational abilities) can reduce the symptoms of these patients to such an extent that over half of them can be brought back to the work force in full employment. One would think that this would be celebrated and supported, but just the opposite happened. The full extent of this tragic farce is told in my autobiography – a work in progress. The short version is that the paying authorities grew weary of paying in the face of criticism from other clinicians maintaining that KLs treatment was not evidence based (true that) and too expensive (relative to what – certainly not in the light of the enormous value of the treatment for the individual patient nor when one considers the value to society of bringing an individual back to the work force instead of languishing on publicly funded income).The short end of the long story is that KL was shot down by the authorities, who refused to pay for services rendered in spite of contractual agreements, which then led to closing down of the activities.

KL never died, though, and I survived by taking clinical work, again. This has led to a further cementation of my Generalist status, but the downfall has taken a serious financial toll on me and my family, which has in turn led to some creative accounting to bring this debt down. It has come so far now that KL is operating again, although in a different guise.

At one of my many conference talks, where I was speaking on the limits of evidence based medicine (believe me, this is a much larger and broader subject than most of us are able to fathom). Meanwhile, at the same conference, I was introduced to a concept called Biphasic Low Level Laser Therapy (LLLT), a treatment for myofascial pain of all types - pains in muscles, fascia and ligaments. Here again, this goes much broader than most of us can fathom, since the main problem with pain in these tissues is not structural, but an inflammatory issue. It is the inflammation that causes adhesion, reduced lubrication and swelling which is why it hurts. KL now offers this treatment on a pay as you go basis, and this is picking up, so that I expect it to be my main activity by the middle of 2013. It is further projected that KL will go out into the world as a leader in non-medical pain treatment with satellite clinics in more and more places as growth allows.

Contact:
Richard Evan Steele, MD, MPH, PDC, BCSPHM
Medical director, Klinikken Livet
Tyttebærvej 26, Sejs, 8600 Silkeborg, Denmark
E-mail: steele@klinikken-livet.dk

ABOUT THE BOOK SERIES
"HEALTH AND HUMAN DEVELOPMENT"

Health and human development is a book series with publications from a multidisciplinary group of researchers, practitioners and clinicians for an international professional forum interested in the broad spectrum of health and human development. Books already published:

- Merrick J, Omar HA, eds. Adolescent behavior research. International perspectives. New York: Nova Science, 2007.
- Kratky KW. Complementary medicine systems: Comparison and integration. New York: Nova Science, 2008.
- Schofield P, Merrick J, eds. Pain in children and youth. New York: Nova Science, 2009.
- Greydanus DE, Patel DR, Pratt HD, Calles Jr JL, eds. Behavioral pediatrics, 3 ed. New York: Nova Science, 2009.
- Ventegodt S, Merrick J, eds. Meaningful work: Research in quality of working life. New York: Nova Science, 2009.
- Omar HA, Greydanus DE, Patel DR, Merrick J, eds. Obesity and adolescence. A public health concern. New York: Nova Science, 2009.
- Lieberman A, Merrick J, eds. Poverty and children. A public health concern. New York: Nova Science, 2009.
- Goodbread J. Living on the edge. The mythical, spiritual and philosophical roots of social marginality. New York: Nova Science, 2009.

- Bennett DL, Towns S, Elliot E, Merrick J, eds. Challenges in adolescent health: An Australian perspective. New York: Nova Science, 2009.
- Schofield P, Merrick J, eds. Children and pain. New York: Nova Science, 2009.
- Sher L, Kandel I, Merrick J, eds. Alcohol-related cognitive disorders: Research and clinical perspectives. New York: Nova Science, 2009.
- Anyanwu EC. Advances in environmental health effects of toxigenic mold and mycotoxins. New York: Nova Science, 2009.
- Bell E, Merrick J, eds. Rural child health. International aspects. New York: Nova Science, 2009.
- Dubowitz H, Merrick J, eds. International aspects of child abuse and neglect. New York: Nova Science, 2010.
- Shahtahmasebi S, Berridge D. Conceptualizing behavior: A practical guide to data analysis. New York: Nova Science, 2010.
- Wernik U. Chance action and therapy. The playful way of changing. New York: Nova Science, 2010.
- Omar HA, Greydanus DE, Patel DR, Merrick J, eds. Adolescence and chronic illness. A public health concern. New York: Nova Science, 2010.
- Patel DR, Greydanus DE, Omar HA, Merrick J, eds. Adolescence and sports. New York: Nova Science, 2010.
- Shek DTL, Ma HK, Merrick J, eds. Positive youth development: Evaluation and future directions in a Chinese context. New York: Nova Science, 2010.
- Shek DTL, Ma HK, Merrick J, eds. Positive youth development: Implementation of a youth program in a Chinese context. New York: Nova Science, 2010.
- Omar HA, Greydanus DE, Tsitsika AK, Patel DR, Merrick J, eds.Pediatric and adolescent sexuality and gynecology: Principles for the primary care clinician. New York: Nova Science, 2010.
- Chow E, Merrick J, eds. Advanced cancer. Pain and quality of life. New York: Nova Science, 2010.
- Latzer Y, Merrick, J, Stein D, eds. Understanding eating disorders. Integrating culture, psychology and biology. New York: Nova Science, 2010.
- Sahgal A, Chow E, Merrick J, eds. Bone and brain metastases: Advances in research and treatment. New York: Nova Science, 2010.

- Postolache TT, Merrick J, eds. Environment, mood disorders and suicide. New York: Nova Science, 2010.
- Maharajh HD, Merrick J, eds. Social and cultural psychiatry experience from the Caribbean Region. New York: Nova Science, 2010.
- Mirsky J. Narratives and meanings of migration. New York: Nova Science, 2010.
- Harvey PW. Self-management and the health care consumer. New York: Nova Science, 2011.
- Ventegodt S, Merrick J. Sexology from a holistic point of view. New York: Nova Science, 2011.
- Ventegodt S, Merrick J. Principles of holistic psychiatry: A textbook on holistic medicine for mental disorders. New York: Nova Science, 2011.
- Greydanus DE, Calles Jr JL, Patel DR, Nazeer A, Merrick J, eds. Clinical aspects of psychopharmacology in childhood and adolescence. New York: Nova Science, 2011.
- Bell E, Seidel BM, Merrick J, eds. Climate change and rural child health. New York: Nova Science, 2011.
- Bell E, Zimitat C, Merrick J, eds. Rural medical education: Practical strategies. New York: Nova Science, 2011.
- Latzer Y, Tzischinsky. The dance of sleeping and eating among adolescents: Normal and pathological perspectives. New York: Nova Science, 2011.
- Deshmukh VD. The astonishing brain and holistic consciousness: Neuroscience and Vedanta perspectives. New York: Nova Science, 2011.
- Bell E, Westert GP, Merrick J, eds. Translational research for primary healthcare. New York: Nova Science, 2011.
- Shek DTL, Sun RCF, Merrick J, eds.Drug abuse in Hong Kong: Development and evaluation of a prevention program. New York: Nova Science, 2011.
- Ventegodt S, Hermansen TD, Merrick J. Human Development: Biology from a holistic point of view. New York: Nova Science, 2011.
- Ventegodt S, Merrick J. Our search for meaning in life. New York: Nova Science, 2011.

- Caron RM, Merrick J, eds. Building community capacity: Minority and immigrant populations. New York: Nova Science, 2012.
- Klein H, Merrick J, eds. Human immunodeficiency virus (HIV) research: Social science aspects. New York: Nova Science, 2012.
- Lutzker JR, Merrick J, eds. Applied public health: Examining multifaceted Social or ecological problems and child maltreatment. New York: Nova Science, 2012.
- Chemtob D, Merrick J, eds. AIDS and tuberculosis: Public health aspects. New York: Nova Science, 2012.
- Ventegodt S, Merrick J. Textbook on evidence-based holistic mind-body medicine: Basic principles of healing in traditional Hippocratic medicine. New York: Nova Science, 2012.
- Ventegodt S, Merrick J. Textbook on evidence-based holistic mind-body medicine: Holistic practice of traditional Hippocratic medicine. New York: Nova Science, 2012.
- Ventegodt S, Merrick J. Textbook on evidence-based holistic mind-body medicine: Healing the mind in traditional Hippocratic medicine. New York: Nova Science, 2012.
- Ventegodt S, Merrick J. Textbook on evidence-based holistic mind-body medicine: Sexology and traditional Hippocratic medicine. New York: Nova Science, 2012.
- Ventegodt S, Merrick J. Textbook on evidence-based holistic mind-body medicine: Research, philosophy, economy and politics of traditional Hippocratic medicine. New York: Nova Science, 2012.
- Caron RM, Merrick J, eds. Building community capacity: Skills and principles. New York: Nova Science, 2012.
- Lemal M, Merrick J, eds. Health risk communication. New York: Nova Science, 2012.
- Ventegodt S, Merrick J. Textbook on evidence-based holistic mind-body medicine: Basic philosophy and ethics of traditional Hippocratic medicine. New York: Nova Science, 2013.

CONTACT
Professor Joav Merrick, MD, MMedSci, DMSc
Medical Director, Health Services
Division for Intellectual and Developmental Disabilities
Ministry of Social Affairs and Social Services
POBox 1260, IL-91012 Jerusalem, Israel, E-mail: jmerrick@zahav.net.il

INDEX

#

20th century, 62
21st century, 81

A

abuse, 57, 77, 123
academic settings, 116
access, xiii, 21, 30, 33, 36, 55, 72, 74, 75, 76, 78, 80, 104, 105, 112
accessibility, 15, 54, 65, 78, 80
accountability, 12, 27
accounting, 7, 37, 120
accreditation, 21
adhesion, 120
adjustment, 36
administrators, 2, 16, 45, 88, 92, 103
adolescents, 71, 123
adulthood, 80
adults, 69, 71, 72
age, xi, 53, 57, 69, 80, 103
agencies, 67, 73
AIDS, v, 62, 124
Americans with Disabilities Act (ADA), 67, 73, 78
appointments, 92
assessment, 56, 71, 72
assistive technology, 76
asthma attacks, 42

atmosphere, 116
attitudes, 22, 88, 91, 101, 103
authority(ies), 6, 8, 12, 14, 16, 28, 30, 32, 33, 39, 40, 59, 73, 88, 96, 97, 119, 120
autism, 71
autonomy, 32, 33

B

barriers, xvi, 8, 46, 72, 79, 80, 89, 90, 91, 93
base, xiv, 15, 28, 30, 112
beneficiaries, 71, 74, 75, 76, 77, 78
benefits, 11, 27, 79
bias, 53
blood, 43, 46, 104
bounds, 16
brain, 71, 122, 123
breakdown, 96
budget deficit, 29
bureaucracy, 116

C

calculus, 67
cancer, 115, 122
candidates, 14
caregivers, 70
Caribbean, 123
cash, xv
central planning, 5

centre practicing physicians, 45
chain of command, 30
challenges, 61, 67, 71
chemotherapy, 115
child abuse, 122
child maltreatment, 124
childhood, 75, 81, 123
children, 42, 53, 57, 62, 66, 67, 71, 72, 80, 115, 121
chronic diseases, 56
chronic illness, 122
cities, 21
citizens, 3, 74, 97
civil rights, 78
civil society, xii
clarity, 4, 28
climate, 95
collaboration, ix, 2, 51, 59, 109
communication, 45, 57, 62, 71, 96, 108, 112, 124
community(ies), xii, 1, 3, 4, 5, 8, 9, 12, 13, 16, 21, 22, 24, 26, 27, 33, 36, 40, 41, 42, 43, 45, 46, 49, 52, 60, 67, 68, 69, 70, 72, 73, 74, 76, 79, 80, 90, 93, 95, 101, 105, 109, 112, 124
community service, 8, 33, 42, 49, 73, 105
community support, 41
community-based services, 76
competition, 3, 5, 7, 30, 60, 61
compliance, 72, 78
composition, 71, 97
comprehension, 79
computer, 46, 112
conception, 107
conceptualization, 19, 29
conference, 60, 120
configuration, 55
conflict, 54, 61
conflict of interest, 61
congenital malformations, 80
Congo, 115
Congress, 3, 4, 67
consciousness, 103, 123
consensus, 27, 35, 88, 111
consumer choice, 68

consumers, 69
control group, 52, 53
conviction, 67
cooperation, 9, 29, 31, 46, 97, 100
coordination, xiv, xv, 2, 4, 5, 19, 25, 29, 31, 40, 43, 46, 75, 96, 99
coronary heart disease, 5, 60
coronary thrombosis, 62
cost, xv, 5, 6, 8, 9, 26, 27, 29, 30, 31, 33, 35, 47, 49, 50, 56, 65, 66, 68, 69, 70, 74, 75, 77, 80, 93, 109
cost accounting, 6
cost benefit analysis, 50
cost containment, xv, 6, 29, 31, 50
cost effectiveness, 50
cost saving, 70
counseling, 70
covering, 30, 61
creative thinking, 119
creativity, xvi
crisis management, 88, 91, 92
criticism, 25, 119
cross sectional study, 63
CT scan, 46
cultural clash, 42
cultural differences, 55
culture, 122

D

daily living, 69
dance, 123
danger, 26, 36
data analysis, 122
data collection, 51, 52, 53
data gathering, 53, 108
data set, 108, 109
database, 12, 46, 47, 51, 54, 55, 56, 81, 103, 104
deaths, 77
decentralization, 27, 53, 95
decision-making process, 11
deficiencies, xiv, 2, 12, 77
denial, 68, 79
Denmark, xiii, 8, 19, 30, 56, 64, 116, 120

dentist, 36
Department of Education, 67, 116
depth, 11
developed countries, 27
developmental process, 85
devolution, 16
dichotomy, 95
direct observation, 23
directors, 30, 96
disability, ix, 28, 43, 65, 66, 67, 70, 71, 72,
  73, 76, 79, 80, 81
discrimination, 77
disease rate, xvi
diseases, xiii, 99
dismantlement, 92
disorder, 71
dissatisfaction, 111
distress, 43
diversity, 2, 6
doctors, xiii, 7, 119
dream, 115
drugs, 50, 108
due process, 78

E

early warning, 23
eating disorders, 122
economic incentives, 32, 66
economic status, 108
economic well-being, 69
economics, 17
ecosystem, xi
editors, 3
education, xi, 43, 45, 64, 73, 78, 100, 108,
  123
educational institutions, 45
educational materials, 79
educational policy, 88, 91
emergency, 33, 41, 46, 77
employers, 38
employment, 45, 50, 68, 69
endocrinology, 43
enforcement, 74, 77
England, 4, 60, 63, 85

English language proficiency, 57
enrollment, 79
environment, 33, 45, 57
epidemic, xii, 66
epidemiology, 107
epilepsy, 80
equality, 33
equipment, 36, 46, 76
estrangement, 5
ethics, 124
ethnic diversity, 72
Europe, xvi, 13, 24, 61
evidence, xi, xiv, 27, 62, 99, 119, 120, 124
exercise, 38, 68, 69, 108
expenditures, 65, 80
experimental design, 63
expertise, 31, 32, 45, 59, 72, 73
exploitation, 77

F

families, 50, 80
family members, 70, 80
fascia, 120
fat, 27
federal agency, 67
federal aid, 80
federal government, 73, 74
financial, xv, 6, 11, 21, 28, 30, 32, 36, 37,
  61, 71, 96, 97, 120
financial incentives, 61
financial performance, 61
financial resources, 22
Finland, 5, 28, 30, 32, 63, 85
first generation, 80
fitness, 80
flexibility, xv, 8
force, 23, 42, 43, 70, 88, 119
free association, 103
freedom, 16, 33
freedom of choice, 33
full employment, 119
funding, xiv, 27, 40, 65, 70, 119
funds, 40

Index

G

general practitioner, 36, 43, 81, 97
generalizability, 15, 54, 55
geo-political, 28
GNP, 28
graduate education, 47
grants, 30, 112
grass, 112
growth, 61, 120
guardian, 53
guidance, 5
guidelines, x, 1, 2, 3, 4, 5, 6, 8, 9, 13, 15, 16,
    19, 21, 22, 24, 25, 27, 31, 33, 39, 40, 46,
    47, 50, 52, 53, 59, 66, 74, 81, 85, 87, 95,
    96, 97, 100, 103, 107, 109, 111, 112
guiding principles, 4, 60, 61, 67

H

healing, 124
health care, xi, xiii, xiv, xv, 2, 3, 4, 5, 6, 7,
    8, 9, 12, 13, 15, 16, 19, 20, 21, 22, 24,
    25, 26, 27, 28, 29, 31, 33, 34, 36, 45, 47,
    49, 50, 53, 54, 59, 60, 61, 63, 66, 67, 68,
    69, 72, 74, 75, 78, 80, 81, 86, 90, 92, 96,
    99, 100, 103, 107, 108, 111, 123
health care costs, 27, 66, 80, 86
health care professionals, 108
health care sector, 29, 33
health care system(s), xiv, xv, 2, 3, 5, 6, 12,
    13, 22, 24, 26, 27, 28, 29, 33, 34, 47, 50,
    53, 54, 60, 61, 74, 80, 90, 99, 100, 107,
    108, 111
health condition, 75
health education, 23, 41, 43, 44, 45, 57, 112
health effects, 122
health insurance, 3, 28, 66, 96
health practitioners, 78
health problems, 23, 80
health promotion, xv, 54, 68
health risks, 80
health services, 2, 6, 19, 20, 27, 43, 49, 50,
    52, 60, 61, 63, 68, 72, 75, 76, 107, 115
health status, 15, 50, 51, 53, 54, 56, 57, 64
historical overview, 6
history, 6, 13, 53, 61, 104
HIV, vi, 62, 124
holistic medicine, 123
Hong Kong, v, 123
hospital sector, 2, 21, 25, 33, 44, 47, 62, 111
hospitalization, xiv, xv, 15, 20, 25, 32, 33,
    34, 35, 40, 50, 85
host, 3
housing, 37, 73
human, x, xvi, 26, 115, 121
human development, x, 121
hybrid, 32
hypothesis, 49, 50

I

ideal, 111
idealization, 112
ideology, 116
immunization, 103
immunodeficiency, 124
impairments, 80
improvements, 36, 75
in transition, 74
income, xvi, 89, 90, 120
independence, 68, 69
individual rights, 79
individuality, 23
individuals, 9, 65, 68, 69, 70, 71, 72, 73, 74,
    75, 76, 77, 79, 80, 87, 89, 92, 108
industrialized countries, 2
inertia, 31
inflammation, 120
infrastructure, 74
injury(ies), 27, 54, 57, 71
institutionalized care, 96
institutions, 6, 37, 43, 44, 45, 59, 68, 73, 90,
    100
integration, 3, 6, 69, 121
integrity, 6, 7, 104
interface, 112
internist(s), xiv, 97
intervention, 23, 52, 54, 68, 103, 112

isolated procedures, 36
isolation, 47
Israel, xiii, 65, 124
issues, x, xi, 2, 4, 5, 7, 15, 20, 54, 57, 60, 87, 88, 95, 99, 112, 116

L

labour market, 9
languages, 116
laws, 11, 22, 31, 69
laws and regulations, 31, 69
lawyers, 97
lead, 11, 16, 32, 35, 73, 96, 103, 116
leadership, xiv, 12, 39, 40, 88, 91, 116
leadership style, 12
learning, 64, 79, 81
learning styles, 79
legislation, 4
lens, 69
librarians, 86
library services, 45
life expectancy, 79, 115
light, 111, 112, 120
lipoma, 43
living arrangements, 43
local conditions, 12, 22, 32
logistics, 17
long-term services and supports, 73, 74, 75, 76
love, xi

M

majority, xiv, 4, 7, 76, 108
man, 36, 50, 99
management, xi, 2, 4, 5, 7, 12, 15, 19, 28, 54, 55, 59, 60, 66, 74, 76, 77, 80, 123
manpower, 13, 31, 32, 33, 40, 41, 63
market share, 37
marriage, 31, 39
mass, 39
matter, 16, 31, 36, 96, 100, 109
measurement, 39

media, 79, 112
Medicaid, xv, 65, 68, 70, 71, 72, 73, 74, 75, 78, 79, 80
medical, xvi, 16, 21, 22, 23, 27, 29, 40, 42, 45, 62, 63, 64, 66, 67, 68, 71, 76, 78, 80, 89, 90, 92, 96, 99, 116, 119, 120, 123
medical care, 63, 64, 78, 90
Medicare, xv, 74, 79
medicine, xiv, 8, 28, 29, 37, 41, 45, 47, 59, 80, 115, 120, 121, 124
membership, 97
mental disorder, 123
mental health, 81
mental illness, 71, 72
methodology, 12, 16, 20, 24, 51, 53, 54, 61, 107, 112
migration, xiii, 123
mind-body, 124
misuse, 42
mobilized resources, 36, 49
models, 29, 32, 33, 40, 80, 88, 92, 103
modifications, 53, 71, 72
modules, 33, 47
mold, 122
mood disorder, 123
morbidity, 35, 62, 77, 80, 99
mortality, 27, 62, 77, 99
motivation, 26, 37, 45, 46
muscles, 120
mycotoxins, 122
myocardial infarction, 42

N

National Council on Disability, 66, 67, 81
National Health Service, 5, 6, 60
national scale, 29, 108
national strategy, 25, 54
needy, 109
neglect, 77, 122
negotiating, 32, 45
Netherlands, 80
neurologist, 66
neuroses, 54
Norway, 30, 45

nurses, xiii, 14, 44, 100
nursing, 21, 22, 36, 37, 43, 44, 45, 90, 92, 97, 103
nursing home, 37, 43

O

Obama, 3, 60
obesity, 80
objective criteria, 39
objectivity, 51
obstacles, 89, 91, 92
officials, 69, 72, 73, 77
old age, 112
operating costs, 7
opportunities, 9, 70, 74, 78
organize, 6
outpatient, 66
outreach, 9, 78
overlap, 22, 54
oversight, 73, 74, 76
oxygen, 42

P

pain, 120, 122
palliative, xi
parity, 74
parole, 5
participants, 8, 16, 39, 54, 70, 72, 78, 79, 87, 88, 89, 90, 91, 92, 93, 111
PCP, 21, 78
peer review, 45, 103
permit, 70
personal communication, 45
personal control, 68
personal goals, 68, 77
Philadelphia, 62
physical activity, 80
physical therapy, 68
physicians, xv, 14, 45, 60, 61, 66, 78, 80, 100, 104
pilot study, 36
platform, 64

pneumonia, 43
policy, ix, 1, 12, 13, 15, 19, 20, 22, 24, 41, 45, 49, 51, 61, 70, 85, 88, 89, 91, 92, 96, 97, 100
policy issues, ix, 1, 15, 45
policy making, 12
policymakers, 28, 74
polio, 66
political power, 31
political system, 31
politics, 27, 124
pollution, 107
pools, 28
population, xv, xvi, 3, 4, 6, 15, 16, 26, 28, 30, 31, 35, 37, 42, 53, 56, 62, 66, 67, 71, 72, 74, 75, 79, 80, 81, 86, 90, 93, 95, 101, 107, 109, 111
population density, 31
population group, 71
positive attitudes, 99
pregnancy, 42, 112
preparation, viii, 19, 42
presidency, 4
president, 67
prevention, xii, 9, 22, 34, 42, 68, 123
primary sector, 4, 8, 20, 21, 25, 33, 42, 63, 89
principles, 4, 51, 61, 66, 81, 124
private sector, 32
problem solving, 44, 46, 92
professionals, 13, 87, 100
profit, 6, 7, 28
project, x, 1, 2, 4, 5, 11, 12, 13, 14, 15, 16, 19, 20, 22, 25, 26, 29, 30, 36, 37, 38, 39, 40, 44, 45, 46, 47, 49, 50, 51, 52, 53, 54, 55, 56, 57, 59, 85, 87, 88, 89, 90, 91, 92, 93, 95, 97, 100, 101, 107, 109, 112
promote innovation, 74
proposition, 1
psychiatry, 43, 123
psychology, 122
psychopharmacology, 123
public health, 3, 5, 6, 7, 28, 29, 33, 60, 86, 112, 115, 116, 119, 121, 122, 124
public interest, 73

public sector, 28, 29
public service, 111
public-private partnerships, 74

Q

qualifications, 45, 88, 91, 101
quality assurance, xiii, 22, 61, 86, 103, 104
quality control, 37
quality improvement, 77
quality of life, 77, 79, 122
quality of service, 77
questionnaire, 56, 57

R

radio, 2, 112
radiotherapy, 115
RE, 61, 62, 64, 81
reactions, 96
reality, 103
recognition, 73
recommendations, 67
recovery, 38
redistribution, 63
reference frame, 22, 24, 25, 26, 46, 89, 95,
    99, 100, 103
reform(s), 29, 31, 60, 68, 75
regionalization, 6
registries, 55
regulations, 22, 97
rehabilitation, 36, 37
Rehabilitation Act, 78
reinforcement, 29
relaxation, 44, 119
relevance, xv, 11, 34, 54, 95, 96, 116
reliability, 51, 53, 57
remedial actions, 77
representativeness, 39
requirements, 44, 73, 74, 78, 79
research facilities, 45
researchers, 59, 121
resolution, 79
resource management, 38

resource utilization, 49
resources, xiv, 1, 8, 12, 16, 24, 29, 32, 33,
    36, 37, 39, 49, 59, 63, 74, 88
response, 54
responsiveness, 32, 119
restructuring, 26
RH, 61, 63
rights, 78
risk, 6, 7, 8, 26, 42, 50, 56, 57, 65, 81, 104,
    124
risk factors, 50, 56, 57
root, 112
roots, 112, 121
rotations, 44
rules, xv, 13, 22, 78, 79
rural areas, 72
Russia, 28

S

sabotage, 68
safety, 76, 77
sanctions, 30
savings, 6, 7, 9, 32, 59, 61, 75
Scandinavia, xii, 31
school, 42, 116
science, xi, 45, 64, 107, 124
scope, 13, 73, 92, 95
segregation, 37
self help, 42, 43
self-worth, 69
sensory access, 78
servers, 55
service provider, 72, 77
service quality, 15, 16, 53, 57, 59
services, viii, xv, 1, 2, 3, 4, 7, 8, 15, 16, 20,
    21, 22, 27, 29, 30, 32, 33, 34, 35, 37, 41,
    42, 43, 50, 57, 62, 63, 65, 66, 68, 69, 70,
    71, 72, 73, 74, 75, 76, 77, 78, 79, 80, 81,
    85, 86, 90, 96, 101, 103, 104, 119, 120
sexuality, 122
shortage, 70, 74
showing, 111
signs, 23, 46
social group, 42

social justice, 5
social network, 39, 41, 43, 108, 112
social services, xiv, 1, 16, 30, 35, 41, 42, 90,
    92, 119
social situations, 37
social support, 28, 37
social welfare, 37, 41
society, 120
solution, 38
specialists, 44, 59, 119
specifications, 74
speculation, 7
spelling, 76
spin, 8, 11, 12, 13
staffing, 43
stakeholders, 67, 70, 72
standardization, 32
state(s), xiii, 3, 7, 11, 32, 55, 65, 66, 69, 70,
    71, 72, 73, 74, 75, 76, 77, 78, 79, 80, 81,
    108
statutes, 79
strategic planning, 9, 19, 25
structure, 9, 24, 25, 28, 33, 45, 46, 95, 104,
    108
style, 80
substance abuse, 72
substance use, 71
substitution, 43
suicide, 123
Sun, v, 123
suppliers, 79
Supreme Court, 4, 73, 78
surplus, 49, 50
Sweden, 30, 45, 60, 116
swelling, 120
symptoms, 8, 56, 61, 64, 119
synthesis, 35

T

target, 4, 15, 22, 35, 44, 49, 52, 55, 56, 90,
    109
target population, 4, 15, 35, 44, 49, 52, 56,
    109
target populations, 52, 56

tax base, 6, 30, 31, 32
tax system, 31, 32
taxes, 30
technician, 44
techniques, 53
technology(ies), xiv, 12, 13, 22, 29, 40, 41,
    46, 77, 99
telephone, 57
testing, 53, 54, 57
textbook, 123
therapeutic procedures, 50
therapist, 44, 112
therapy, 122
threats, 51, 77
trade, 17, 51, 59, 111
trade agreement, 17
traditions, 57
training, xiv, 17, 36, 44, 45, 69, 70, 76, 79,
    100
training programs, 100
translation, 55
transparency, 55
transplantation, 16
transport, 42, 105
transportation, 73, 78, 90
treatment, xiii, xv, 8, 23, 30, 37, 41, 43, 54,
    61, 62, 76, 88, 89, 101, 103, 115, 116,
    119, 120, 122
trial, 52, 62
true/false, 37
tuberculosis, 124

U

ultrasound, 46
uninsured, 3
unions, 26, 30
United Kingdom (UK), 60, 79, 80
United Nations, xii
United States, 3, 60, 62, 65, 66, 67, 80, 81,
    96
upper respiratory tract, 54
urban, 36

V

vaccine, 66
vacuum, 52
valuation, 104
variables, 26
vector, 112
vertical integration, 7
victims, 66, 68
visions, 85
vocational rehabilitation, 73
voting, 31

W

wages, 9, 69
waiver, 73, 75
war, xiv

Washington, xvi, 60, 63
water, 27
weakness, 7, 27, 36, 54
wealth, 39, 103
welfare, 37, 43
well-being, 67
wellness, 68
Western Europe, 27
White Paper, 30, 62
WHO, xii, 4, 5, 14, 20, 22, 60, 61, 62, 63, 64, 107
wholesale, 26, 85
workers, 44, 70
working conditions, 42
workplace, 70

Y

yield, 70